To Ridhwan and Istafiah

Thank you for all
your wisdom and support.
May the Tao be with you!

Ahmad Anthony Miles

TAO OF WELL-BEING

DEDICATION

This book is dedicated to
Muhammad Subuh Sumohadiwidjojo
and
J. R. Worsley
without whose inspiration
this book would never have been written

ACKNOWLEDGEMENTS

I would like to thank Kathryn Barnwell, my editor, whose insights and unwavering support for the purpose of this book, made my job easier and more meaningful as we went along.

I wish to thank Branka Hrgovich, the designer of the book, for her creative awareness and practical suggestions in making the look of the book match its contents.

I wish to thank Joshua Paul Malkin for the hours of conversations that helped shape the content, focus, and presentation of this work.

I wish to thank all my patients over the years whose life experiences made meaningful and real the subject of this work.

I would like to thank all those ancient Chinese men and women whose deep explorations of human life and purpose were the guiding structures for the creation of Tao of Well-Being.

Lastly, I would like to thank Helen Franklin who said, "Where's the book?"

Introduction

As a practitioner of classical acupuncture for thirty years I have seen people from all walks of life who, in one way or another, have been faced with significant disruptions of their lives. I would argue that the fundamental issues raised by people are issues of the spirit. Their questions are: What is happening to me, and where do I go from here? At a certain point it seems that the usual way of doing things doesn't work anymore. It is as if the clothes of their lives do not fit, but there are no new clothes to replace the old ones. It is an existential dilemma that is very painful, frightening and isolating.

It seems that many people feel they have "lost their way". When I say that I have "lost my way", I may mean several different things:

- that the way in which I have been walking has become difficult or impossible to maintain
- that my journey through life feels like a burden weighing me down
- that my path has led to physical illness that has made me question my preconceptions and past priorities
- that my path has led me away from others and I feel like a stranger in a strange land
- that I can't find my way home
- that I no longer have a clear destination in mind
- that I have strayed from a path that has been laid out by those who have come this way before.

All these "losses" are upsetting to equilibrium, disturb well-being and seem to demand some remediating action. In our modern, materialist world, well-being tends to be described in terms of actions and outcomes, and health is seen as the result of activities such as exercising, learning, connecting and so on. Accordingly, when I have lost my way, I need to do something: look around for a path, realign myself with my goals, improve my fitness levels. But can we really assume that a focus on external; activity will produce internal benefits such as happiness or a sense of well-being?

In our time, where we are faced with challenges and possibilities never experienced before on this planet (as far as we know), we need to draw on resources that can truly support us in the most holistic ways. We need the depth and range of consciousness available from all wisdom sources past and present to aid us in finding our own unique sense of well-being. Purely materialist approaches that serve only the body and the mind, ignoring the spirit and the soul, are of limited use, and may even contribute to our feeling of having "lost our way".

At first glance the world of the ancient Taoists is a mystery to our modern eyes. However, when we look more closely, we find that they see us very clearly and very compassionately. They already knew what we would be up against, and, most importantly, they offered us a way to move forward where there seemed to be no way forward, no obvious path, no next step. They showed us a way to gain or regain our true path. Consider this conversation that Zhuangzi, ancient Taoist, imagines taking place between Confucius and Laozi on the subject of how to teach rulers how to rule:

Confucius to Laozi:

"I completely mastered the six classics - the Songs, the Book of History, the Rites, the Canon of Music, the I Ching and the Spring and Autumn Annals. I then met seventy-two rulers, expounding the Way of former Kings. Not one of them was interested! Not one!"

Laozi replied:

*"You were lucky that no ruler took you up on it! Those six classics are the dusty old paths of ancient Kings. They tell us nothing of **the force that guided their footsteps**. (My emphasis). All you expounded was their dusty old paths. Paths are made by shoes, but they are not shoes."* (Zhuangzi, 28)

When Laozi talks about "dusty old paths", he is referring to a focus on the external, the material world that preoccupied the Confucians. The Taoists were less interested in the thought//insight/activity that was produced, and more interested in "the force that guided" the production of that thought/insight/activity. They were more interested in the inner processes than the external production.

In order to evaluate true well-being, we need to understand how "the force that guides" affects the way we engage with life. For the ancient Taoists, this meant engaging with a process based on what they considered to be true principles that applied as much to the health of a community and its leadership as it did to individual well-being. Indeed, for them, proof of the validity of the underlying principles was the fact that they applied to every aspect of human life. The primary question the Taoists asked was not "**what** should I do?" but "**how** should I do?" The "how" is addressed in the Neijing, The Yellow Emperor's Classic of Internal Medicine which is the oldest medical text we have from the ancient Chinese, probably 3,000 years old. The book is a series of conversations between Huangdi, the Yellow Emperor who was the legendary founder of Chinese civilization, and his physician/teachers, especially Qibo. Here is Huangdi's first question and Qibo's answer:

Huangdi:
"I have heard that in ancient times people lived to be over a hundred and still remained active and energetic. But people nowadays start to fail when they get to fifty. Is this because the world is changing, or is it because human beings are neglecting the laws of nature?"

Qibo:
"In ancient times people who understood the Tao patterned themselves on yin-yang and lived in harmony with the universe developing practices to promote the qi, and inner work to connect with the cosmos. They used moderation in eating and drinking. Their sleeping and waking were regular and orderly. They did not over-stress their bodies or their minds." (Neijing, 97)

The Taoists believe that if we focus on how best to live, the outcomes will take care of themselves. Qibo focusses on people who *"understood the Tao"* and who *"pattern themselves on yinyang"*. In other words there were true principles that were based on reality. Reality inspires meaning and guides perspective as well as generating the force that creates external activities such as medicine, exercise, meditation and leadership. Taoist thought sees that everything is about context, process and relationship. Through principles such as *yinyang*, the Taoists believe we are able to be in relationship with reality, the great generative field of unknowable potential that underlies all life.

Western understanding of reality has traditionally been based on a separation of humanity from nature. Nature actually means life, that which "is". So the terms "nature", "life" and "reality" are interchangeable. Since we are also nature, the separation of ourselves from nature, is the separation of ourselves from ourselves. Nature, life and reality, observed as quantifiable, material, objective qualities become something to be manipulated, controlled, or denied. Relationship, which is the core process of the Taoist approach, is irrelevant in this world view.

For the Taoists there is no separation of the human from the rest of nature, no separation of mind and body, no separation of self and other. Everything is an expression of interdependent relationships. The Taoist perspective is an ecocentric rather than an anthropocentric perspective and is being reassessed in the West, primarily because advanced Western scientific thought, especially in the cutting-edge life sciences, understands that "reality" is all about self-sustaining networks of interdependent relationships. Fritjof Capra, physicist and author, offers this comment:

"At the forefront of contemporary science, we no longer see the universe as a machine composed of elementary building blocks. We have discovered that the material world, ultimately, is a network of inseparable patterns of relationships; that the planet as a whole is a living, self-regulating system. The view of the human body as a machine and of the mind as a separate entity is being replaced by one that sees not only the brain, but also the immune system, the bodily tissues, and even each cell as a living, cognitive system. Evolution is no longer seen as a competitive struggle for existence, but rather as a cooperative dance in which creativity and the constant emergence of novelty are the driving forces. And with the new emphasis on complexity, networks, and patterns of organization, a new science of qualities is slowly emerging."
(Capra and Luisi, xi)

The focus on outcomes is a focus on results - Laozi's *"dusty paths"*, rather than *"the force that guides"*. In the *Tao Te Ching*, thousands of years old and perhaps the single most influential philosophical work of the ancient Taoists, supposedly composed by the legendary Laozi, the *"force that guides"* is accessed through the process of engaging with reality. The *Tao Te Ching* says:

"once you find the centre and achieve harmony,
heaven and earth take their proper places
and all things are fully nourished".
(Chung Yung, as qtd. in Zhuangzi, 4)

Laozi's emphasis on *"finding the centre"* implies enquiring into our relationship to the centre. Life becomes meaningful when we discover how to go beyond what the Taoists called 'acquired conditioning' - the life that results from our biography and our survival patterns - and regain connection with our 'original nature', *yuanshen*, in effect, our destiny. So, well-being concerns the process of cultivating our relationship with our original nature and finding guidance from within.

The context for the Taoist process is the understanding of reality, or true principles. Reality is the context for well-being. Since reality is always something beyond what we think it is, what is it we need to understand and do in order to engage with reality? And why is this important? For the ancient Chinese there were fundamental principles or qualities that were the basis for the understanding of reality and essential for well being. Chapters One to Eight, Understanding Reality, will explore these qualities. They include:

> *tao (the way)*
> *wu (the empty centre)*
> *yin yang*
> *xin (the heart)*
> *wuxing (the five elements)*
> *wushen (the five spirits)*
> *nature*
> *heaven and earth*
> *ming (destiny)*
> *yuanshen (original nature)*
> *wuwei (knowing without knowing)*
> *zhi (knowing-how)*

In order to engage with reality - an internal, rather than an external process - we must begin at the start, at the place which is the invitation we have received to bring our consciousness into play, that is: our suffering. Suffering is life. Suffering and well-being are like magnets irresistibly drawn to one another. Suffering is the catalyst for well-being; well-being is the virtue, the implicit value and purpose of suffering. My prayer for my children used to be," May my children never suffer, but may they suffer". There is no development without suffering. From suffering can emerge consciousness which can then begin the transformation of suffering into well-being.

When we "lose our way", we become aware that we need to re-orient ourselves. This is the first invitation sent by our suffering: awareness. The following chapters will explore true principles, suffering and the transformation of suffering and will describe the strategies and tools necessary to engage with reality, suffering and well-being at what I call The Meeting Place.

We are all pilgrims on the journey. Our inner nature demands that we finally find the path to who we truly are. Heartbreak, illness and identity crises are the catalysts we use to arrive into the territory of ourselves. Once we arrive into the territory of ourselves, what is the way we can use that can help us find our way through it? I call this way - the Meeting Place. The Meeting Place is not an esoteric notion, it is a generative theme that applies to everything about our lives from the most mundane to the deepest, inner place within us; from cleaning our teeth to communing with God. It is as accessible as breathing, because it is life itself - and we all have experienced it. We have just never named it, and therefore have not consciously been able to use it to find or rediscover our true path. The Meeting Place is the unstated path at the heart of all Taoist practice. It is the Tao of the Tao.

Close your eyes. Place your tongue on your upper palate, breathe in gently, slowly, through your nose. Pause at the top of the breath for a moment, then, breathing through your nose, breathe down deep into your belly, sending every part of yourself down into your depths. Pause before the next inhalation. Repeat this three times. You will notice how different you feel from when you started. Open your eyes. Just three simple breaths and reality changes. You will feel more present, more in the moment. You are in touch with what the ancients called the Tao.

Chapter One
Understanding Reality: Tao

"Humans follow earth
Earth follows heaven
Heaven follows Tao.
Tao follows its own nature."
(Tao Te Ching, trans. Mitchell, chapt. 25)

TAO

The first context central to the Taoists' engagement with reality was the understanding of *Tao*. What is *Tao*? For the Taoists of ancient China it was a way of engaging with the nature and purpose of life itself. They would argue, though, that once you begin writing about it or talking about it, you have already lost it, because it is always beyond our reach, beyond the duality of the mind! This is a fundamental paradox. Nevertheless, the monumental Taoist classic, the *Tao Te Ching*, was still written down, somewhere around the third millennium BCE. Following humbly in the footsteps of Laozi, and for the purposes of this book, we can identify ways of looking at the *Tao* which can point us in the direction of that which cannot be described! The *Tao* is simultaneously many things depending on one's particular focus at any one time. As much as it might be considered a "way", it also seems to be identified with the notion of *Wu* where *Wu* represents the empty centre or field of potential, the unknowable mystery at the centre of life. *Wu* manifests in time and space as *Tao*. *Tao* can be expressed as:

1. Tao as the unknowable mystery

In positioning the mystery of existence as the meaningful centre of a life with all its challenges, its ups and downs, its surprises and gifts, Laozi describes the process in this way:

> *"We shape clay into a pot,*
> *but it is the emptiness inside*
> *that holds whatever we want.*
> *We work with being,*
> *but non-being is what we use."*
> (Tao Te Ching, ch.11)

If we can place mystery, non-being, at the centre of our understanding of life, if we can allow supreme meaningfulness to the unknowable and of all that we do not know, then our 'knowing', our lives, will be aligned with cosmic and earthly truth. Our inner lives will be rich, free, unconventional and authentic, and our outer lives will contain our true contribution to our community and our world, adding value to human life. In other words we will be living in the Tao; we will be healthy.

2.   Tao as Origin and Return

> *"In the beginning was the Tao.*
> *All things issue from it;*
> *all things return to it....*
> *To find the origin trace back the manifestations.*
> *...Use your own light*
> *and return to the source of light.*
> *This is called practising eternity."*
> (Tao Te Ching, ch.52)

Before everything there was the *Tao*. The Taoists focus on consciousness as a tool to help us return to origin, to the before. For them consciousness was not the goal, the goal was the return. One of the five limitations we impose on ourselves (discussed in the section on suffering) is the importance placed on time-related life changes such as birth, growth, maturation, waning, death. The inner work and training of the Taoists was to reverse the entropic process by aligning themselves with eternal principles and practices that could transform the material reality of the body itself at the cellular level. This process led to greater longevity and health, but primarily was the way to align with the *Tao* and return to origin.

3.   *Tao* as the oceanic field of potential.

The *Tao* is the supremely meaningful void at the centre of life itself. It is the unknowable no-thing at the centre of something. It is as if our material bodies with all their densities of bone, organ tissue, blood and so on are filled with openings of light shining and sparkling through our bodies, giving direction, meaning and beauty to the most ordinary aspects of our lives. The scientific examination of matter produces smaller and smaller entities at the core of which is a void, an empty centre. The *Tao* is that empty centre, a field of benevolent potential, around which life revolves.

> *"There was something formless and perfect*
> *before the universe was born.*
> *It is serene. Empty.*
> *Solitary. Unchanging.*
> *Infinite. Eternally present.*
> *It is the mother of the universe.*
> *For lack of a better name*
> *I call it the Tao."*
> (Tao Te Ching, ch.25)

4. *Tao* as Totality

Everything is about totality, everything is a part of and contains everything else. "As in Heaven, so on Earth" would be an appropriate Taoist mantra. In the qigong work there are three axes. The breath inside me is my personal axis. At the same time, the axes of the cosmos and the planet, the Pole Star and the mythic Kun Lun Mountain, also run through me. These axes interact and influence one another. In reality they are all one. Everything is in everything else. It is an interactive, interpenetrating, interconnected field of potential. The Taoists have always known this, and modern science is now catching up.

5. *Tao* as Manifested Divine

The Taoist perspective sees no separation of the spiritual and the material. To paraphrase Lori Eve Dechar in her book, *Five Spirits*, itself a great and inspiring contribution to the understanding of Taoist classical work, it is as if the whole of existence is a spiralling vortex - at one end, the fine radiance of the spirits, at the other end, embodiment and the dense materiality of a rock. Everything is part of everything else, moving back and forth, resonating, vibrating, pulsating through the spiralling vortex. For the Taoist this meant that everything is accessible, there is no separation, no thing-in-itself. Everything is about relationship. Everything, including our relationship with everything, is the divine made manifest. *Tao* is the divine. *Tao* is the meaning of existence.

6. *Tao* as Existence

"The Tao is the way things are,
from which you cannot depart
even for one instant.
If you could depart from it,
it would not be the Tao"
(Chung Yung, as qtd. in The Second Book of the Tao, 2)

Tao is the golden and silver breaths breathing everything into being. *Tao* is equated with life itself. It is the mysterious root and generative means of life. We exist, therefore we experience *Tao*.

7. *Tao* as Non-Attachment

"People who study the Way first must recognize reality and unreality before they can enter the Way. We have seen actors portraying failure and success, gain and loss, parting and meeting, sadness and happiness; their outward forms are as they appear, while their minds are inwardly calm. What have they attained that they are able to be unmoved in mind like this? They are clearly aware that these representations, the costumery and the makeup, the states of mind and the life situations, are artificially created - they switch and shift roles without loss or gain to themselves. Learners can understand the Way by contemplating this."

(The Cultivation of Realization, author unknown, 14th century C.E. as qtd. in Taoist Meditation, trans. Thomas Cleary, 41)

Attachment to external situations (eg. success) and internal states (eg. happiness) necessarily means a lack of freedom. If I am attached, I can no longer relate. Furthermore, lack of freedom prevents us from accepting what is. When we cannot accept what is, we are out of alignment with ourselves, one another, the planet and the universe. We fill ourselves with agendas and expectations and then find emotions and circumstances are running us. We are no longer taking responsibility or leadership in our own house.

8. *Tao* as Way.

"Open yourself to the Tao,
then trust your natural responses;
and everything will fall into place."

(Tao Te Ching, ch.23)

Tao as Way assumes that through patience, trust and willingness we will be directed to an appropriate life, and we will know this. In knowing this, we can accept what comes our way and work with it. Trust and willingness support an embodying process of knowing. Tao as Way produces deep core knowing.

Summary

All the elements of the Tao listed above centre around how to live life. The Tao is the most fundamental principle when we wish to ascertain well-being. It is best summed up by a quotation in The Essence of Wisdom:

"A monk once asked Zen Master Yun-Men, 'What is the essence of the Supreme Teaching?'
Yun-men said, 'When spring comes, the grass grows by itself.'"
(The Essence of Wisdom, 100)

Going to the Meeting Place - the central concept of this book - is the practical experience of the Tao. All the aspects of the Tao can be experienced through the practice of the Meeting Place. In effect the Meeting Place is the Tao of the Tao. As preparation for engaging the Meeting Place, we must first understand what the Taoists mean by reality and the place of suffering in our lives.

Chapter Two
Understanding Reality: Yin Yang

"Yin/Yang is the Tao of Heaven/Earth
It is the common thread of the ten thousand things
The father and mother of change and transformation
The beginning in which life and death are rooted."
(Neijing, chapter 5, as qtd. in Larre, Schatz and Rochat de la Vallee, 55)

Yin and Yang are familiar words to most of us now. For the ancient Chinese they were a fundamental principle of engagement with reality, and, for the purposes of this book, of engagement with well-being. Yin and Yang represent the transformative and integrative processes of life in a state of creative, dynamic tension. Yang is the infinite within us, the formless within us, the breath, the creative, the imagination, the conscious mind. Yin is the finite within us, the form within us, the receptive, the manifesting, material body. Without the movement back and forth between Yin and Yang, all life ends. The West has designed a culture which separates us from nature. It has separated Yang from Yin. As a result there can be no flow, because there is no 'between', there is no relationship, there is no Meeting Place where yin and yang engage.

Because we in the West have interrupted the flow of Yin and Yang, we have made life a catastrophe not only socially and ecologically, but also within our own individual beings. This is why there is so much illness and distress in our modern world. The ancient Taoists looked at the many ways in which Yang and Yin are naturally expressed, and naturally and unnaturally cultivated, in human society. This book, with its emphasis on Taoist perspective and the central focus of the Meeting Place, is an invitation to, and a strategy about how, to reclaim the dynamic tension of Yin and Yang.

1. YIN YANG AND THE SEASONS

"The alternating concentration of yin and yang
Produces the seasons."
(Huainanzi, ch.7, as qtd. in Larre,63)

Winter is absolute yin, dark, quiescent, still. The spring is characterized by yang advancing, an upward, fast, forceful movement, and Yin retiring. In spring the days are longer and warmer, the plant emerges from the earth into light. In the summer yang completes itself with the full expansion of the day, the maximum heat and light, the flower at the peak of bloom, colour and fragrance. In the late summer, yang begins to retreat and yin to advance. The days shorten, still hot, but the nights are colder. There is a condensing quality manifesting in the ripened fruit. In the autumn the yin advances further, the yang retreats further, the days grow shorter and colder, the sap descends into the root, the leaves fall and decompose. We can look at our day as a seasonal cycle in the same way: the morning is spring, noon is summer, afternoon is late summer, dusk is autumn, night is winter. And so the cycle repeats itself.

Every season in the cycle, every period of the day is inevitable and necessary. What a teaching for us if we could ebb and flow, receive and release as Mother Nature does! What a transformation of our lives if we understood and acted in harmony with this reality, instead of trying to bend the natural cycle to our will!

2. YIN YANG: THE INTEGRATION OF THE CELESTIAL AND THE MUNDANE

"Real knowledge is all real.
But it needs to be espoused by conscious knowledge.
Refining away the yin of acquired conditioning,
the two become one whole."
(Chang Po-Tuan 983-1082 C.E., Understanding Reality, trans. Thomas Cleary, 6)

Taoist thought entertains many ways of looking at Yin and Yang, one of them being the flow of the seasons described above. Another was to look at the actual dynamic of Yin and Yang in practice. The Complete Reality Schools of Taoism, emerging in the late 10th century C.E., viewed Yin and Yang as key ingredients in the work of spiritual alchemy. For these Taoists, Yin represents the experience of the everyday mundane world, Yang the world-transcending higher consciousness. Since we tend to begin the engagement of the integration of yin and yang after temporal conditioning has embedded itself, and the 'mundane' has dominated the 'celestial', we need to focus on practices that "repel yin" and "foster yang".

In addition this practice needs to ensure that we successfully embed the celestial in the mundane, that is, achieve what I call 'the monastery in the marketplace', the integration of the inner and outer aspects of our lives. Zhang Sanfeng, Complete Reality Taoist from 13th century China and originator of Tai Ch'i Chuan said:

"The teaching of spiritual alchemy says that when the mind runs off one should gather it in; having gathered it in, then let go of it. After action, seek rest; finding rest, one develops enlightenment. Who says one cannot find tranquility in the midst of clamour and activity?" (quoted in the Taoist I Ching, edited by Thomas Cleary, 16)

I see the cultivation of the monastery in the marketplace as an important step in our modern world. It cannot simply be an attitude, it needs to become embodied at the cellular level and in daily social interactions. In my practice I see the result of the lack of integration of the inner monastery with the outer marketplace, of the inner and the outer. Seeking external, outer solutions to inner challenges is a dead end, yet this is what we are often offered, for example medication to deal with deep spirit states such as depression, anxiety, despair, hopelessness, fear. The deep harm this causes to the spirit shows itself in all kinds of psychosomatic conditions and the anxiety and terror resulting from a lack of meaning and purpose.

What does 'fostering yang' look like? Creative self-expression, self-contemplation, reaching deeper, the examination of dreams, visiting what inspires, seeking mutuality, are some of the ways to 'foster yang'. The key way is through "the meeting place", which is discussed in a later chapter. The integration of Yin and Yang combined with the emphasis on the cultivation of the Yang, the celestial, seems an increasingly urgent require-ment to help us all through these challenging times.

3. YIN YANG: INNER MOVEMENT/ OUTER MOVEMENT

One more useful way of looking at the Yin Yang re-lationship is in terms of Yang as the outer-moving reality or experience, and Yin as the inner-moving reality or experience. Yin Yang is usually presented as a circular image. The circular image is an abstract, static description of complementary oppo-sites. In real time and space it needs to be configured as a figure eight, or the symbol of infinity.

CREATIVE

RECEPTIVE

In the outer movement of Yang we experience something in our engagement with life which is then brought internally through the inner movement of Yin, perhaps as a feeling, a sensation, a thought. Ideally everything is processed through a never-ending loop of outer into inner, inner into outer. What tends to happen is that some Yang experiences are so difficult to process when brought in through the Yin that they get stuck in the inner Yin state, and block the continual loop of inner and outer movement. Suffering of some kind halts the process, and as a result we lose some of our vitality, our life force, which needs a clear, clean field of potential in which to operate. The flow needs to be uninterrupted.

Creative engagement with our own suffering - for example, through movement, voice, writing, painting - dissolves the "stuckness" in the Yin and liberates the vital force, the qi, to continue expressively into the Yang. The point where the four directions of Yin and Yang intersect is the fifth element, the organizing principle of life, the *Wu*. By engaging creatively with our suffering we activate this organizing principle and the flow is restored.

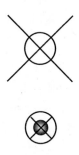

4. YIN YANG: YIN EMBODYING YANG

If we look at our lives, we can see how Yin and Yang work together, complement each other. Without the Yin process of sleep we cannot do the Yang process of awake. The Yang upward rising of my foot is followed by the Yin downward descending of my foot. And yet in our Western culture we put a lot of value and emphasis on the Yang, far less on the Yin. External activity, business, timetables, achievement, success, doing, doing, doing. In fact, there is nothing inherently wrong with such activities. The outer creative force with its dynamism, its intention and strategies is an absolute requirement of life. Yet without the inner creative Yin force of holding, integrating and strengthening the truth, the benefit of the Yang experiences cannot be integrated into ourselves. That integration occurs through our bodies. So we end up doing a lot in the outer and depleting ourselves in the inner. We become like dried-up wells. We use everything up but do not restore it, and, significantly, are unable to learn at the cellular level and in our conscious minds what life needs to teach us.

My teacher, J. R. Worsley, told me once, *"You are serving everybody but yourself. I want you to take a three mile walk every morning. Serve yourself first, and you will be able to serve everyone else"* (clinical notes). I had been exhausting myself with all my activities without a corresponding focus on replenishing myself. The all-out Yang pattern results in depletion, so we crash. Crashing becomes the extreme choice our bodies take to integrate the Yang within the Yin. How often do we get sick at weekends or holidays, times when we can integrate into the Yin?

In our culture Yin tends to be explored more through crisis - illness, suffering, loss - rather than through inner exploration, inner training. The benefit and value of the Yang activity cannot be gained without the integrating process of the receptive Yin. It is the integrating process of the Yin that embodies the Yang value of our activity. A doctor once said to me, "*For every hour in the workplace, an hour in the forest*". Yin and Yang are a natural dynamic in our lives. When we consciously engage in maintaining the balance of Yin Yang, we tend to be healthier, and more engaged with the purpose and value of our lives.

Yin Yang through the seasons, Yin Yang through the integration of the mundane and the celestial, Yin Yang through the flow of the outer-inner, Yin Yang through the Yin integration of the Yang experience, all provide useful contexts for our relationship to reality, moving us beyond the "wandering" human mind to the "shining" mind of the Tao.

Chapter Three
Understanding Reality: Heaven and Earth

"Incubated by Heaven and born by Earth,
the 10,000 things are complete.
Of these, the most precious is the human being."
(Neijing, ch.25)

The ancient Chinese described themselves as the Hua, the flowery, splendid people, of the Chung-kuo, the Middle Kingdom. China was the Middle Kingdom because of being surrounded by barbarian worlds, but also because 'middle' is the meeting place of Heaven and Earth. Out of Heaven - the One, flowers Earth - the ten thousand things, which are the endless material expressions of Heaven. Heaven and Earth then interact. Out of the love-play of Heaven and Earth comes a precious and significant element - human beings. Heaven is the celestial, spirit-bearing force in us. It is our potential, our consciousness, our rationality, our imaginative and creative forces moving beyond form. Earth in us is our somatic experience, our material existence on the planet. It is the manifestation of form and of time. Heaven is everything that is infinite about me, Earth is everything that is finite about me. It is from this place of meeting between Heaven and Earth, called the "middle void", that we flow. In seeing ourselves less as a materialized object and more as the continuously transforming expression of the play between Heaven and Earth, we will be closer to reality.

For the ancient Chinese human beings are "precious" because they are highly evolved. They are highly evolved because of the presence of the spirits, the *Shen*, within them. Earth provides the irresistible means for the Heavenly presences, the *Shen*, to incarnate. Heaven provides Earth with the transformational potential of the *Shen*. The human being is the pivot through which Heaven and Earth can spin their endless dance and manifest in the ever-evolving uniqueness of human destiny, *Ming*.

In the *Neijing* the author describes the relationship of Heaven and Earth in the human microcosm as the relationship of the *Jing* and the *Shen*. The *Jing* are the earthly essences structured through the kidneys, the *Shen* are the heavenly forces that descend and dwell in the Heart. The same name, the shao yin is given to both the heart and kidney meridians. The *Jing* irresistibly attract the animating force of the *Shen* and the *Shen*, the spirits, respond to the *Jing*, the form. This process is mediated through the heart, the organizing principle of life.

The ancient Chinese character for the heart indicates a container, open at the top to receive the *Shen*, but also all the influences that determine life. The heart holds the space and is the space. The *Shen* and the major influences on our life move freely in the space provided by the leadership of the heart and, as a result, *"we can have all the profound, deep movements of being which are in the realm of the mind and the psyche which will guide your life, and which are physical as well as mental"* (*The Heart,* Claude Larre and Elisabeth Rochat de la Vallee, 59). Without an understanding of the interplay of Heaven and Earth, well-being becomes a distant echo rather than the glorious call that it is.

Through the dynamic of Heaven and Earth we can see ourselves as a process rather than a product or a fixed me. And not only a process, but a process that, through its authentic dynamic, leads us into our destiny, our *Ming,* becoming more and more of what and who we really are. When we are engaged in authentic process, then ming means that circumstances change and evolve in accordance with our purpose. This concerns circumstances within our body, mind and spirit as much as our external lives. Instead of desperately trying to figure everything out on our own, subject to external pressures and attractions, we realize we are part of something much bigger, that there are dynamics moving through us which we can trust.

The experience of aloneness, of sadness, is the experience that comes from the lack of connection to the process of Heaven and Earth. The feelings of anxiety, despair, depression have relevance as feedback on the disconnect between Heaven and Earth within us. The more we can join with reality, with Yin Yang, and Heaven and Earth, the more we become both the dancer and the dance. Standing strongly between Heaven and Earth we are naturally in relationship. In the felt reality of relationship the experience of aloneness evaporates. We find that we know what to do, how to move; thoughts and feelings come naturally and appropriately; our physical internal processes start to move in accord with their true nature rather than being yoked into directions based on fear and anxiety. The ancients called this *wuwei*, knowing without knowing:

> *"Not knowing is true knowledge.*
> *Presuming to know is a disease.*
> *First realize you are sick;*
> *then you can move towards health.*
> *The Master is her own physician.*
> *She has healed herself of all knowing.*
> *Thus she is truly whole."*
> (Tao Te Ching, ch. 71)

From the perspective of the ancient Taoists and classical medicine we are hardwired only for transformation. We are not hardwired for comfort, nostalgia, sentimentality or material focus. We are an alchemy whose work is the transformation of all our 'lead' into 'gold'. The interplay of Heaven and Earth is the process of life and therefore of transformation.

In the names of acupuncture points we find constant reference to the transformational process. For example, the Liver point, *Middle Seal*, indicates two aspects: The first, '*Middle*' indicates our essential place between Heaven and Earth; the second, '*Seal*' is the symbol of divine authority. This point is about carrying out the Mandate of Heaven as a true human being. *Palace of Weariness*, a point on the Heart Protector meridian, has two aspects. The first is *Palace* which indicates the highest level of existence within us, the abode of the gods, the palace. The second aspect, *Weariness*, concerns the insult and injury to the our Heart through life's challenging journey. So the point's purpose is to give our Heart a spiritual shower, to clean off all the muck and debris, and set it on its true path of inner transformation.

When we spend time in Nature, we can experience the meeting of Heaven and Earth within us. It feels like a deep peace, a deep breath, a collapse of the vigilance into a softness in our eyes, a feeling that there is nothing for us to do because everything is being done. Our voices soften and quieten, our laughter comes more easily, we stop and listen, and when we listen, we can feel we are being listened to. Standing amongst the great trees that are our elders, we experience appreciation of detail, deep knowing, limitless sense of being. We smell the forest, we hear the listening, we see that we are being seen, we touch what touches us. We are amongst our own kind, where we truly belong: between Heaven and Earth, pouring eternally and limitlessly out of the middle void into the Life within the life.

Chapter Four
Understanding Reality: The Heart

The ancient Chinese Heart is different from the modern western heart. The Heart in the west is a material object, a pump governing the blood and the blood vessels. Although the ancients recognized the physical heart, they had a more complex and richer sense of what it was really about. The pump is the physical manifestation of its essential function. Its essential function is to provide a home in the human being for the Shen sent from Heaven to guide us through their radiance, that that bring the value of the infinite into our finite life.

The ancient character for the Heart shows an empty space at the centre of a bowl open at the top. When the Heart is serene and tranquil, it is a welcoming irresistible invitation to the *Shen*. *"The Heart is the rooting of life, the place where changes are made by the Spirits"*. (Neijing, chapt. 9) The Spirits radiate out from the heart everywhere there is life.

The Heart is like a deep mountain lake where nothing ripples the surface, no unnecessary movement disturbs its stillness. This emptiness and stillness at the centre, *Wu*, is the organizing nexus for the whole of life. *Wu* is always potential, and the Heart is the mechanism of that potential in us.

"The Tao has neither root nor stem, no leaf nor flower,
but all ten thousand things are born of and grow from it.
It comes to rest in the compassionate Heart.
In the tranquil Mind and harmonized Qi is where the Tao abides."
(Guan Zhi (770 - 476 BCE) as qtd in Johnson. Chinese Medical Qigong
Therapy, Volume I, 46)

The Heart is the means by which we know the *Tao*:

"How can a person know Tao? By the Heart.
How can the Heart know?
By emptiness, the pure attention that unifies being and quietude.
The Heart is never without treasure, yet it is called empty....
The Heart is alive and it possesses knowledge, it knows,
and from knowledge makes distinctions.
To make distinctions is to know all parts of the whole at once."
(Xunzi, 313-238 B.C.E., as qtd in Rooted in Spirit,
Claude Larre and Elisabeth Rochat de la Vallee)

Master Xun is talking about the energetic heart, and even more, the heart within the heart. *"In the centre of the heart there is another heart"*, (Guanzi, ch.49, The Art of the Heart, 7th Century B.C.E., as qtd in Larre, The Heart, 83). This inner heart is the innermost part of the inner, as far as it can go, fathomless and limitless within our individual being. *Wu* is the potential and the heart is the field of potential through which all life manifests and can be known.

When the Heart is agitated, the *Shen,* the radiant and beautiful birds of Heaven for whom the Heart is the resting place, fly away, leaving us directionless, broken, despairing and, more than anything, void. Zhang Jiebin (1563-1640 C.E.) comments:

"When the Shen are overwhelmed, they leave; when left in peace, they remain. Thus the most important thing in the conduct and treatment of a being is maintenance of the Shen, and then comes maintenance of the body."

(as qtd. in Larre, Rooted in Spirit, 33)

When the *Shen* can maintain their home in our hearts, our destiny unfolds and our direction becomes clear through the illumination of the *Shen* within us.

How do we support the mutuality of the *Shen* and the Heart? In other words how does life become meaningful? It becomes meaningful when it embodies the truth. It embodies the truth when we find how to go beyond what the Taoists called 'acquired conditioning' to regain connection with our 'original nature', in effect the life of the soul.

In Chapter five of the Xi Ci, the Great Treatise on the I Ching, the Classic of Change, it says:

"That aspect of the Tao which cannot be fathomed in terms of the light and the dark is called Shen."

(I Ching, The Great Treatise, 301)

The *I Ching* is based on the two fundamental principles of light and dark, the principles which represent yin and yang. *Shen* is something that cannot be explained in terms of duality, of the interaction of yin and yang. *Shen* is the unfathomable divine *"which must be revered in silence"* (I Ching, chapt. 5, Great Treatise). So *Shen* exists beyond duality, is transcendent and immanent at the same time. Since the Heart is the dwelling place of the *Shen*, it contains some of the quality of the Shen in its function of medium for the *Shen*. This is described in the Neijing:

"What is the spirit? The spirit cannot be heard with the ear. The eye must be brilliantly perceptive, the heart must be open and attentive, and then the spirit is suddenly revealed through one's own consciousness. It cannot be expressed through the mouth; only the heart can express all that can be looked on."
(The Yellow Emperor's Classic of Internal Medicine, trans. Ilza Veith, 222)

So, well-being concerns the process, the way of cultivating meaning from the dynamic of *Shen* and Heart. As such, well-being is the experience of the *Tao*.

In classical Chinese medicine we find another aspect of the Heart. The Heart, as the central agent of the Fire element, *Hou*, is called *'the Supreme Controller who rules through Love and Understanding'*. What this means is that the body, the mind and the spirit cannot function without being ruled by unconditional love and understanding. The organs, the nerves, the blood, the bones, the mind and the spirit, everything has to have the Heart as sovereign and ruler, otherwise it will not function properly. The Supreme Controller, the Sovereign, is the organizing principle of life, the power that makes our lives human and creates meaning. The Sovereign takes everything to its highest purpose.

The primacy of the Heart Meridian is noted by being described and numbered as the first meridian. It is no accident that the first point on the Heart Meridian is described as Utmost Source, that is, that which, at the level of finite life on earth, is closest to the infinite root of everything. The Heart straddles the finite and infinite worlds. In this sense, it is distinct from all other parts of us and for this reason, within the ancient work, there were practitioners who did not needle the Heart Meridian or Channel, and, while there are twelve dominant meridians, only eleven are mentioned in some texts.

In addition, the ancient Chinese described the Heart as the home of the mind. Its name is *Xin*, sometimes translated as heartmind. So the Heart receives the *Shen* but also organizes the psychological life of a human being in accord with the forces of the *Shen*, themselves the guides from Heaven. When the Heart is disturbed, the mind is disturbed. The ancient Chinese character for the Heart is found in the foundation characters of attributes of the mind such as purpose, will, thought and reflection.

These three aspects - the Spirit-welcoming field of potential, the qualitative organization of consciousness and life, and the incarnation of love - characterize what the ancients mean by the Heart. And the Heart is central to the notion of

Well Being. So the support, maintenance and empowering of the Heart will consequentially organize life, including life in our bodies, in ways that are appropriate, meaningful and authentic.

> *"For the mind in harmony with the Tao*
> *all selfishness disappears.*
> *With not even a trace of self-doubt,*
> *you can trust the universe completely.*
> *All at once you are free,*
> *with nothing left to hold on to.*
> *All is empty, brilliant, perfect in its own being"*
> (Seng-Ts'an - 606 C.E. from The Mind of Absolute Trust, as qtd in Mitchell,
> The Enlightened Heart, 27)

When the Heart operates as the centre, the field of potential for the organization of life, then it cannot be attached. Non-attachment manifests in the Heart as appropriateness or propriety. Non-attachment is the authentic nature of the Heart: the Heart as the open field of potential through which all experience can pass: experienced but not held in a clinging embrace.

How do we know the attachment within the Heart? Through inappropriateness. When we "take things to heart", when something has become too personal for us, when someone slights us - a thoughtless remark, a critical tone, an irritated response - and we find ourselves going into hurt, when we feel a weight, an ache, when we feel cold, unsafe, uneasy, uncertain, angry, in these moments we are attached to whatever external focus is providing the charge.

The need to be liked at all costs or the belief that we are unlovable is a biographical issue. It often starts in childhood. The love we need to feel loved, to flourish, to feel safe, to feel accepted, to feel known, may not have been available or accessible. The lack of love is the worst attack we can face. It is too much for the Heart to handle. We become extremely vulnerable and everything becomes very personal.

The initial lack of love in our biography can eventually become an internal dynamic, something perpetuated without any cause outside of our body, mind and spirit, telling us we are not loveable. Events can trigger old trauma. We can even generate external circumstances which actually make us disliked to prove we are not loveable. When the Heart is called on again and again to protect what has now become a self-generated attack, it can get worn down and, with the Heart exposed, we face the greatest danger to our body, mind and spirit. The distress of the heart can then lead to major issues with the physical organ itself. Indeed, cardiovascular disease is the leading cause of death in the European Union, the U.K., the USA and Canada.

Zhuangzi's perspective on non-attachment described below is still helpful.

"If a man is crossing a river
and an empty boat
collides with his own boat,
he won't get offended or angry,
however hot-tempered he may be.
But if the boat is manned,

he may flare up, shouting and cursing,
just because there's a rower.
Realize that all boats are empty
as you cross the river of the world,
and nothing can possibly offend you."
(Zhuangzi, Mitchell, The Second Book of the Tao, 20)

The problem, presented in the first stanza, is met with a strategy, presented in the second stanza. Understanding reality involves understanding the Heart. The subtle, deep and powerful force that the ancients describe as the Heart is a far cry from our impoverished modern understanding. Instead of a core that is solid and separate, the ancient Chinese offer us a field of potential based on relationship, spirituality and love. We have always known the truth of this; it is in all our music, poetry, dance and art. We whistle, hum and sing it through our day. We chant it in our temples and churches, our mosques and monasteries. We feel it in our touch, it lights up our eyes, it quickens our pulse, it's there in our quiet appreciation of nature, in our laughter, in our compassion.

Chapter Five
Understanding Reality: Ming/Destiny

"My nature is what I am, my destiny is to become what I am."
(Chinese text unknown)

"The privilege of a lifetime is to become who you truly are."
- C. G. Jung

Long life means *"the pursuit of the perfect working of a being who, according to their nature, completes the measure of their destiny and dies in their own time"*
(Claude Larre, Elizabeth Rochat de la Vallee, Jean Schatz, Survey of Traditional Chinese Medicine)

Destiny is the *Tian Ming*, the Mandate of Heaven, conferred on us at birth. Life is to carry out that mandate but it is our choice whether we do. When we align ourselves with the *Tao*, with *Yin Yang*, with Heaven and Earth, we will naturally carry out *Ming*. Fate occurs when we have not joined with the Mandate of Heaven. Then we are subject to the arbitrary play of external influences. We become resigned and lose our grasp on life. The world of acupuncture points abounds with names which indicate this connection with *Tian Ming:* Gate of Destiny, Heavenly Window, Spiritual Soul Gate, Soul Door, Spirit Seal, Receiving Spirit, Heavenly Pivot, Heaven Rushing Out, the list goes on and on. We are designed for the highest, most complete expression of ourselves. When we join with that destiny, when we join with what is, when consciousness allies itself with existence, we have the most powerful means for the creation of the well-being of body, mind and spirit.

Ming also assumes that our life through our destiny is intimately linked to the laws of Nature, to the existence of the cosmos itself, and to one another. Human beings are considered the pivot, almost a midwife, between Heaven and Earth, facilitating the flow of the infinite and the finite forces of life. Heaven communicates through the *Shen*, using our hearts to earth itself. Earth, overseen by the Heart and facilitated by the *Po* - *"the wise depths and animating forces of the body"* (Dechar, 240) -organizes itself to receive the contact with Heaven. The result is our individual destiny.

In our modern time we have lost contact with the Mandate of Heaven and, therefore, our destiny. We are dominated by *Po* disconnected from their relationship with the *Shen*. The result is a focus on our desires, a preoccupation with our psychological unease and subjection to illness, where everything is effort. My acupuncture teacher, J. R. Worsley, said that, despite higher levels of physical care and nutrition, we have just as much disease as in the past. Materialism has impoverished our lives, reducing us to fragmented, disconnected entities. The effort required to maintain such an unnatural lifestyle has resulted in exhaustion and sickness. Depression, anxiety, claustro-phobia, self-doubt and loneliness are accompanied by violence, abuse, hedonism, entitlement and narcissism. Even for those who maintain a human balance in their lives, the effort to do so can become exhausting. The ancient Chinese approach, with its focus on eternal principles as relevant today as in the past, can help us engage with our own destinies and thereby transform this state of affairs.

Chapter Six
Wuxing/ Wushen - The Five Elements/ Five Spirits

五行

*"When the spiritual energies of the five elements are assembled,
the Great Tao may be obtained."*
(Chang Po-Tuan, qtd. in Understanding Reality,)

The Five Elements - *Wuxing* - describe the process of
life from conception to death. The elements form a cyclical
progression. They are characterized as water, wood, fire, earth
and metal. Each element transforms into the next element in
the cycle - water becomes wood, wood becomes fire and so
on. Each element has many correspondences including body
organs, colours, sounds, aromas, emotions, tastes, seasons,
directions, climates, body parts, sense organs, zodiacal animals
and planets. The Water, Wood and Fire elements are the rising
energies of the appearance, development and maturation of
life; the Earth, Metal and Water elements are the descending
energies of the condensing, transformation and ending of life.
Water contains both the beginning and the end of the life cycle.

The dynamic of change through the five element cycle

illustrates that, once again, human beings are a fluid purposeful process, a cycle, rather than any one thing. Everything is about relationship and transformation. What follows is a brief description of the elements themselves, particularly their inner aspect, the five spirits, *Wushen*, which shape our transformational process.

Shui/Zhi Water

 Water is the process of fluidity in us, that which is impossible to nail down. It is our flexibility. Water always seeks the deepest level, so water is the depth within us and the capacity to go to depth. It is our reservoir, our reserves, our extra that we can draw on when the challenges come. It is our resilience, our immune system, our capacity to endure. It is also our capacity to protect. It is the foundation of our house. It is the power that drives everything along in us; the power to wash away pollution. It is our will and determination to engage with destiny. Water is a vast, indomitable force, which cultivates in us the appropriate use of our resources. It is our wisdom. It is the essence of ourselves. It asks the question - who am I?

Mu/Hun Wood

 Wood is our energy rising, our movement, our dynamic process of transformation. It is our assertive vitality, our vision and imagination. It is our sense of purpose, our flexibility of mind and body. It is our growth according to our nature. It is our sense of hope, our kindness and sense of justice, our capacity to embrace the new and the unknown. It is the powerful movement of becoming. It is our capacity to think, to plan and execute, to organize, to create. It is our assessment and our judgment. It is what gets us up in the morning, it is the spring in our step, our optimism. It is the future within us. It asks the question - where am I going?

Huo/Shen Fire

Fire is our love and joy at the accomplishment of our hopes and dreams. It is everything at its peak. It is our relaxation and our enjoyment. It is our appropriateness. It is the sense of freedom, the feeling of being at one with all. It is our energy and our enthusiasm. It is our communion with the divine mystery and our understanding. It is the power behind the capacity to transform ourselves. It is our lightness of spirit, our laughter, the capacity and impulse to pour love into everything. It provides the ease for the flow of ideas and feelings, for the intimacy of our deeper relationships. It is our empathy, our intuition, our love. It is the present, the being here in this moment now. It asks the question - am I present in my life?

Tu/Yi Earth

Earth is what is beneath our feet, our sense of home, of belonging. It is the feeling of peace that comes from being stable, grounded on the earth. It is our capacity to nourish and be nourished, the

Mother within us, the devotion within us. It is our solidity, our sense of security in knowing that what we have sown, we have reaped. It is the satisfaction of achievement. It is our capacity to transform energy into matter, our capacity to process food, ideas, spirituality. It is our intention. It is our sympathy and compassion and our sense of balance; that what we express and what we receive are two sides of the same coin. It is our sense of being centred. Our Earth holds and contains us like a mother's embrace. It asks the questions - do I belong and where are the possibilities for transformation?

Jin/Po Metal

 Metal is the sense of value and quality in our lives. This sense of value comes from the connection to the divine spark through whose purity and essence our lives are enriched. Metal is our capacity to receive the new and release the old, to receive what we truly need, and to release what no longer supports us. It is our capacity to be inspired. It is the sense of correctness, and the constitution of moral and spiritual authority in our lives. It is the Father within us, the guide, the authority and the wisdom. It is the unconscious depths of ourselves through which we gain our sense of value and preciousness. We talk of precious metals. The image of Metal is gold within the earth. It is embodied wisdom. It asks the question - what is precious about life?

The Five Elements are life and constitute the vital organization of a human being's existence. *Wuxing/Wushen* pivot around the *Wu*, represented by the number 5, also called *Wu*.

ancient   modern

The ancient character for the number 5 shows the upper half as heaven, the lower half is earth. The number 5 is the meeting place of the heavenly and earthly forces, the intersecting point in the middle of the character. The empty centre, the *"middle void"* of the *Neijing*, is that from which we human beings come. The elements are five in number because the truth of the five manifests in them.

Wuxing work with two dynamics, the sheng cycle, the life or creative cycle, and the ke cycle, the control or limiting cycle.

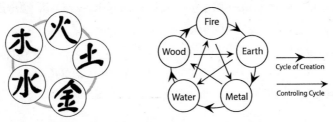

In Lorie Eve Dechar's Five Spirits, she talks about the *Sheng* cycle preventing the *Ke* cycle from endlessly limiting form to the point of cosmic destruction, and the *Ke* cycle preventing the sheng cycle from endlessly creating form to the point of cosmic suffocation. *Sheng* and *Ke* are there to create a dynamic equilibrium, themselves another example of the play of *Yin/Yang* and heaven and earth.

As *Sheng/Ke* the *Wuxing* dynamic is about the relationship of energy (formlessness) and form, of expression and containment. Out of the formlessness of the void comes material life which is then transformed back into formlessness. That is why the Taoists can talk about being and non-being as aspects of reality. Problems occur when this relationship breaks down: form is no longer appropriately animated, energy is no longer appropriately contained, and chaos ensues. The relationship is broken in our lives when the survival patterns of our acquired conditioning successfully resist the movement towards the authentic self. How many times can we say 'No' to ourselves, before we start to crumble from exhaustion and despair?

"As acquired conditioning runs affairs, mundanity increases and the celestial retreats, day after day, year after year. Inwardly, myriad thoughts cause trouble; outwardly, myriad things coerce. Under inward and outward attack, the celestial energy wanes away and the whole being becomes totally mundane... the life forces cannot be sustained, and death is inevitable."
(Liu I Ming's Commentary, as qtd. in The Inner Teachings of Taoism, Chang Po-Tuan, 67).

The endless transforming cycle of the Five Elements creates and maintains life. The qualities of the elements described above and the *Sheng/Ke* pattern are the content of this cycle. In the work of spiritual alchemy, the elements are perceived in yet further dynamics in order to pursue the process of inner transformation. I mention this only to stress the significance of the Elements in Taoist work. The process of spiritual alchemy will be addressed in a further work. What is important for our enquiry into well-being is the relevance of these qualities and patterns and how they aid us in our need to understand reality. The Five Elements take on a more tangible form in the next chapter, The Five Seasons.

Engaging consciously with the Five Elements and the Five Seasons naturally leads us to an exploration of the Meeting Place of nature with life itself. When we look at ourselves and one another through the lenses of the Elements and the Seasons, we find a perspective that is particularly useful in our engagement with our emotional and psychological life, and with the organization of our lives through the year.

Chapter Seven
Understanding Reality: The Seasons

The Seasons are a useful way to look at how Yin and Yang work in our natural environment and in our lives. *"Do not fail to observe the ... seasons"* advises the *Neijing.* The Five Elements or Five Phases - water, wood, fire, earth, metal - have many correspondences. The ancient Taoists had a holistic perspective that saw the essential relationship between every-thing on earth and beyond. One of the ways the ancient Taoists used to look at themselves was through Nature. Today we tend to look at Nature as environmental wallpaper or as something to protect. For the Taoists it was essentially a teacher, a guide. They saw the relationships between the movement of the stars and a blade of grass. The seasonal cycle, because it was a cycle transforming itself, changing constantly within immutable 'nat-ural law', provided a significant lens through which the Taoists observed human life.

There were two aspects of Nature which interested them. One was its cycle of transformation and the other was the identifying characteristics of each season. In relation to the cycle they observed that death in Nature was only a necessary stage in a living process - without the rose dying, there would be no more roses; that everything was to do with relationship - each season developed organically from the previous one, that the Spring was the Mother of the Summer and the Summer the child of the Spring since it came out of the Spring; and that each season was a part of the whole, that there was no hierarchy of importance between the seasons and between each season and the totality - everything was equally important. The Taoists believed that there was an order in nature, a natural law that governed the flow and myriad manifestations of Nature, the seasonal cycle being a prime example. They examined how that natural law works within us.

The second aspect was to be found in the function of the season itself and the way that function is also inside us. Each season emphasizes certain qualities that are in us all the time. Each season asks us to pay particular attention at that time to these qualities so that we are in alignment with Nature and with ourselves. Whatever is outside is also inside.

WINTER - the Water element in Nature

The winter is characterized by its internal depth and power. In the winter the qi of the plant, the sap, is primarily focussed in the root, in the depth of the plant, protected and safe from the cold and extremities of the season, committed to being born again, enduring, powerful. In the winter there is root growth. It is in the depth of the earth in winter that the new life begins, in darkness that the seed sprouts. New life is born from and within darkness, not light. The light will eventually nourish it along with the earth nutrients and the rain, but the seed, the new life, as it is in us, is born in the darkness, from the unknown, the oceanic mystery of life. As Laozi says in *Tao Te Ching*, ch.1,

> *"Free from desire, you realize the mystery.*
> *Caught in desire, you see only the manifestations.*
> *Yet mystery and manifestations*
> *arise from the same source.*
> *This source is called darkness.*
> *Darkness within darkness.*
> *The gateway to all understanding."*

The winter brings a silence to Nature. The absence of material in the atmosphere, (such as insects, pollen and so on), produces a clarity, an emptiness in which sound travels far, nothing in the way. For us it is also a time for clarity, simplicity, for self reflection, to turn down the volume of the outer life with all its demands and to listen to the silence within. The winter invites us to sit within and quieten ourselves.

In the winter we see everything in its essence. A deciduous tree, for example, is reduced to its basic structure, its trunk and branches, and we see clearly its fundamental self without the leaves, the flowers or the life in and around the tree. The winter in us is also our essential self, our root being, our core. How we fare in the winter is a good measure of our state of health, since in the winter we have no support from the elements. We draw support primarily from within ourselves.

The winter in us is the depth within us and the capacity to go to depth, to plunge below the surface and draw on power lying deep within us. It is our capacity for perseverance, preservation, self protection and safety. It is our will, our endurance, to move through the challenges of life and keep emerging as ourselves. It is our immune system, our reservoir, our well.

The ancients encourage us to 'sleep more, work less' in the winter in order to conserve energy for the spring. Since Yin is the quiet depth, resting nourishes the Yin. In our modern world it means doing the least we need to do in order to get something done. Just as our society is typified by waste, so within our bodies we mirror that same waste. As much as we might be concerned for the outer environment, the economic utilization of resources, the ecological footprint of our culture - we must also attend to our inner environment, the economic utilization of our inner resources, our inner ecology.

Our winter encourages us to develop resources, supports for our journey through life. Some of these resources are internal - how we view life - and some are external - what we build into our life to support it. The key winter resources are the internal ones, the self-sustaining, power-generating resources that support the development of the self, the enduring power of the Yin. These allow us to face the challenges of life, its heartbreaks and disappointments, its requirements and demands, without being rocked to the foundation.

How resilient are you? Are you strong in your sense of yourself? Do you meet the challenges or do you succumb to them? Do you feel shaky? Do you feel overwhelmed? Do you catastrophize? Can you be comfortable with people disagreeing with your decisions, your actions, your choices? Do you have a spiritual or inner practice? Do you take time for retreats, for silence, for reflection, even for mindless gazing? Do you enjoy solitude?

SPRING - the WOOD element in Nature

The essence of the spring is Yang, upward-moving transformation but transformation according to a purpose. The purpose is to make manifest what something is meant to be. The spring's transformative power takes something growing and hibernating inside the earth and brings it upward beyond the earth into the light. When we look around, we see how deter-mined is Nature to carry out this plan.

When we hold a seed in our hand, what we really hold and see, is what that seed will become. We hold the future. The spring is the new beginning for the previously dormant plant. It begins to fill and occupy its space. A plant that does not have the proper space to flourish, grows gnarled and twisted.

The spring in us is this transformative power, the capac-ity to change. But it is not any change, it is change according to our true purpose, the purpose of realizing ourselves as authentic human beings, realizing our destiny. In the spring, our eyes come alive because there is so much more to see. The spring is our capacity to express ourselves creatively, to organize and plan out our lives. It is our visionary sense, the sense of possibility, potentiality, of fulfilling ourselves. It is the Yang force in us arising out of the hibernating Yin of the winter.

It is our sense of self-regulation and self-expression. Without clear regulation and expression we cannot take our rightful place. In this sense it has a lot to do with justice, with what is required to claim our space. The acupuncture meridian of the gall bladder, the function of which, together with the liver, that connects to the spring, runs through all the major joints in the body. It enable us to move where we wish to move; to change and transform through movement.

When the spring is not alive within us it manifests in deficiency and excess. In deficiency we can find ourselves mired in depression, with little sense of possibility, devoid of imagination. There is a sense of hopelessness about life. We cannot see what to do or how to do. We can feel frustrated, apologetic, intimidated and bewildered by life. We can lack the courage to face the challenges of life, preferring to sidestep, avoid, be inappropriately conciliatory, engage in passive-aggressive behaviour, not take our rightful place, complain, become the timid victim.

In excess we can be quick to anger, intolerant of any obstacle to our desires. We can bully and be abusive, overriding other people's wishes or interests. We can be arrogant, rigid in thought - 'the rules are the rules'. We can be unkind, cruel, wishing to dominate. In excess we lack humility, are inconsiderate, and suffer high levels of frustration.

The Taoists characterized the energy of the spring as "assertive vitality". We in the West have translated assertive vitality as "anger". What we call anger, the Taoists see as a reaction to the restriction or denial of "assertive vitality". Assertive vitality is not aggressive, but that capacity in us to step forward, to offer our view, to challenge injustice, to stand strong for what is true, for our communities as much as ourselves. It is the force to occupy our own space. When we are denied that space, especially as children, and are forced to be silent and to comply, forced to follow others' agendas, the anger turns inward, tensing the jaw, grinding the teeth at night, restricting vocal expression. The result is a tightness of speech, a whispering or a shouting voice and a sapping of vitality.

Either way there is pressure put on the Heart, the summer child of the spring Liver, and the Heart is starved of what it needs. The 'anger' of assertive vitality nourishes the Heart, gives it room for expansive expression to celebrate life. In the *Neijing* the Spring in us is characterized in this way:

"One paces in the courtyard with great strides,
Hair loose, body relaxed,
Exerting the will for life;
To give life and not to kill,
To give and not to take,
To reward and not to punish.

This is the way that is proper
To the qi of the Spring."

Do you organize your life around your priorities? Do you tend to procrastinate? Can you see beyond yourself to a larger good that makes you larger? Do you have clear boundaries? Do you have the courage to walk your talk? Do you spend any time imagining what your best life looks like? Can you say,"no"? Do you have a vision of what your life is about? Are you Waiting for Godot? Are you curious and inquisitive? Do you ask questions? Do you challenge authority? Do you listen? Do you spend time thinking? Do you engage in creative pursuits? Have you taken the path?

SUMMER - the FIRE element in Nature

In the summer the Yang reaches its maximum extension. Growth slows down, plants spread, flowers bloom, crops ripen. Warmth, the beauty and the profusion of sounds, tastes and fragrances of Nature characterize this season. The days are longer so that everything can absorb as much solar heat as possible. However, too much warmth, too much heat can cause plants to shrivel and die, and too little can cause stunted growth. The heat has to be just right - it has to be appropriate.

The summer in us is characterized by warmth and love. On summer days we naturally relax in nature, spending enjoyable time with others, take holidays. It is natural to let the qi flow freely outside at this time of year. We have more time to be with one another, more time for sharing, for intimacy, for fun and pleasure, for connection at every level. With the warmth everything flows more easily, more fully.

When the Summer in us is strong, we can give and receive love, we can celebrate life, we can laugh, we can feel the depth of our bonds, we can immerse ourselves in the intimacy of our relationships, we can function appropriately according to circumstance, not giving too much attention, not giving too little. We can be empathetic, compassionate, accepting, supportive. The internal function of the summer is the Heart. The Heart is at the centre of life. It is no accident that all four meridians that relate to the Heart all flow through the arms and the hands. Through the hands we connect. A better name for the hands would be 'Tools of Love'.

When the summer in us is deficient, we can experience ourselves as alone, not able to give or receive love. We struggle with relationship, we fear intimacy, we are challenged by sexuality. We are reluctant to trust, avoiding eye contact, touch. Even our voices can sound devoid of life, empty. Our eyes lose their sparkle, our mouths turn down, our bodies sag and cave in. We can become dismissive, negative. We take everything personally.

When the summer is in excess, our behaviour can become inappropriate. It might express itself in indiscriminate sexuality, indulgence in any excess with few moral boundaries. We can develop a fierce intensity, a fanaticism of the body, mind or spirit. We do not love, we only desire. We wish to possess without relating. We dream of fires out of control. We can be cruel, manipulative, harmful.

The summer is the full and true manifestation of ourselves in our lives. The voice is the expression of our Heart, the internal function of the summer. We are designed to speak the truth since the Heart can only speak the truth. When we feel obliged to lie, to pretend, to boast, to fabricate, to speak through the mask, it is an indication both of the suffering of the Heart and an attack on the Heart at the same time. The summer within us is the solar power, the radiant warmth of the Spirits illuminating our awareness, connecting us to creation, the joyful embrace of being.

Do you enjoy your life? Are you comfortable sharing feeling? Do you easily express yourself? Can you be spontaneous? Do you laugh a lot? Do you ever smile when you're alone? Do you have really good friends? Can you cry? Do you wake up in the morning feeling eager to enjoy another great day? Do you dance, do you sing, do you paint or write, do you share, do you stay in touch? Are you discriminating? Can you keep a confidence? Do you invite? Do you ever experience deep peace? Do you experience wonder? Do you feel communion with God and Goddess, with the Creator, with the Universe, with the Mystery? Can you be playful? Are your hills alive with the sound of music?

LATE SUMMER - the EARTH element in Nature

In the late summer the Yang starts to lose its force and the Yin starts to advance a little. The late summer is characterized by abundance and the sense of nourishment. By this time, flowers start to fade but fruit ripens, and once again the Earth, Mother Earth, gives us nourishment for our survival. Some of my first images of coming to Canada were images of abundance: the Niagara peninsula with all the fruit and vegetable stands, the back lanes of Vancouver with trees heavy with fruit, ripe for the picking. The Earth is the mother of everything that lives, spreading nourishment everywhere, spreading seeds everywhere. In times past the harvest ensured survival through the Winter. When crops failed, starvation loomed. We, like all living creatures, depend on the earth for our survival. She is our Mother whose generosity is revealed in the late summer. She is our home, our place of belonging.

The late summer in us is the sense that life is abundant, that life nourishes us from birth to death. It is also a measure of our investment in life. If I invest wisely, if I grow the crops that nourish my body, mind and spirit, then I will reap the benefit, I will receive my harvest. It is the Mother in me. No matter what my biological mother was like, the Mother in me is the part that can care for my well-being; it is the part that grounds me. It is the sense of safety and belonging, of this life as home. It is my capacity to pay attention, to notice, to listen, to think. It produces a profound gratitude, a caring attitude to all around me. I become somebody who is reliable, consistent, available without self interest, caring without attachment, without expectation, without an agenda.

When late summer is deficient within us, we can feel like a motherless child crying out for attention that never comes. We have sown but no harvest has come. We may be well nourished in the body, but spiritually skeletal, unable to feel the connection with the life force within and around us. We worry about everybody. We can be divorced from our bodies (a common occurrence in Western society) caught up in our thinking and worrying, unable to accept what is. We can easily spin off into chasing one idea after another, no thought actually embodying itself inside us, but drifting away on the winds like a cloud. We can feel that nobody cares, feel sorry for ourselves, believe that others, ultimately God, are to blame. And blaming is what we do. We are powerless in the face of Fate.

When the late summer is in excess within us, we involve ourselves in everybody's affairs, interfering in people's lives without any invitation on their part. Care-taking as an agenda is personified in the overattentive parent. Our responses of care will tend to be inappropriate, bringing the focus on to us rather than the person or issue at hand. We become narcissists, the ones who do everything, even good deeds, to garner attention and be acknowledged. We become martyrs, resentful of people's lack of appreciation for all that we do. We feel it is our responsibility to take care of everyone else while putting ourselves last. Every act is conditional. Whether deficient or in excess, the result is a lack of true nourishment or sense of belonging.

The body is our home while we are here. Not the body in the sense of a biochemical entity, but the body in the sense of a miraculous material force that can contain, express, and be transformed by the spirit and the soul. We know that body, mind and spirit are one and that the late summer in us, our Earth Mother, is central in that transformation - spirit into energy into material being.

How nourished do you feel by yourself, by relationships, by your work and your work culture? Do you continually sacrifice yourself on the altar of necessity or expediency, business and familial obligation? Has time become a tyrant rather than a door endlessly opening for you? Are you easily bored? Do you feel at home at home? Are you grateful for your life with all its ups and downs? Are you comfortable in your body? Do you like your body? How do you give back to your community? Do you feel you belong? Can you enjoy your own company? Are you reliable? Do you get things done? Can you bake your cake and eat it too?

AUTUMN - the METAL element in Nature

The movement into autumn, like the movement into spring, is a very dramatic one. The Yang is rapidly retreating and the Yin rapidly advancing; days are colder and shorter, sap descends into the roots. In spring we move from the hibernation of winter into the wake-up call of the spring. In the autumn Nature tells us that the magnificence and abundance of the summer-late summer periods are all over for another year. Whatever beauty and abundance it has established, nature lets it go. There is decisiveness about it. No matter how good it has been, it is finished now. I remember as a child playing out late with my friends in our avenue and my mother calling us in for a bath and bed. "But, Mum", we would cry, "Can't we stay out a little bit longer? Pleeeease!". Our cries would fall on deaf ears. My mother, like the autumn, commanded us to come in and that was that. The autumn is the time of letting go. It is also a journey of the sap into the root, where the sap will be protected from the cold, dark winter.

The autumn is a time when Nature moves from form into formlessness. The leaf decomposes into the earth. For the Taoists it was always a most amazing mystery how Nature could go into formlessness in the Autumn, and then somehow reconstitute life from the seed sprouting deep down in the earth in the Winter. They revered that mystery, referring to it as the "mysterious pass".

The decomposition of the leaf, the collapse of form, at the same time is essential for benefit to be given or acknowledged, since the decomposed leaf then enriches the earth, increasing the capacity for healthier plant life, never mind all the beings living in the earth and benefitting from this process.

The autumn in us is characterized in the same way. The process of letting go, of cultivating non-attachment, is essential in the development of meaning. When we are not attached, we can engage fully and freely, and relate. Through authentic relationship we develop awareness and understanding. When we cannot let go, we become mentally and spiritually constipated, hanging on to old grudges, old beliefs, resistant to new possibilities, insistent that we are right, critical and condemnatory of alternatives. Do we want to be right, or do we want a relationship?

Just as the sap descends towards the root, so we 'descend' in the autumn. I call it the pilgrimage to the source. In the Autumn our gaze turns more inward. The ancients talk about yin advancing and yang receding. The Yang is our outer life, the yin our inner. When we go within, we let go of the outer, of the world, and we become more sensitive, more vulnerable to the inner deeper reality, the inner meaning of life. All meditative practices encourage this autumnal process within us. If our lives are filled with busyness and expression, with no time for quietness and reflection, we begin to wither inside, feeling claustrophobic, burdened, tense, sighing, fatigued. Our autumn needs its time too! It's about balance, the balance of the yin and the yang. We are both, and without one we cannot really be the other. We are better at the outer than the inner, even though our spirits crave for the sustenance only the inner can supply. There is nothing more satisfying than a walk in the autumn, few words being spoken, just the feel and smell of the leaves beneath our feet, the glory of the autumnal colour, the emptiness of the air, being being. There is nothing more satisfying than that moment with ourselves, where the breath comes all of a sudden, like a deep, beautiful sigh, descending down into the depths of our belly, the journey home.

The 'mysterious pass' in ourselves is explored in many different ways in the Taoist world, especially that of inner alchemy. It is at the heart of the understanding of the *Tao*:

> *"Return is the movement of the Tao.*
> *Yielding is the way of the Tao.*
> *All things are born of being.*
> *Being is born of non-being."*
> (Tao Te Ching, chapt. 40)

> *"(The Tao)...is hidden but always present.*
> *I don't know who gave birth to it.*
> *It is older than God."*
> (Tao Te Ching, chapt.4)

The autumn in us is this place of no-thing at the core of our something; it is a radiant space embedded in the material matrix of life. Because it has no form, it is not limited. It is the source, catalyst and the direction for healing and meaning. The Buddhists say you have to take the path, and when you get to the end of the path, you realize that you were there all the time, but you cannot know this without taking the path. The autumn in us directs us along this path.

Do you appreciate yourself? Can you receive appreciation from others? Do you have a sense that life has meaning, that life is worth living? Are you a critical person? Can you let go of the past? Do you hang on to old grudges, old wounds? Are you receptive to new ideas, to others' ideas? Do you find it uncomfortable to be uncertain? Are you comfortable with ambiguity? Are you respectful to yourself? Do you acknowledge your own birthday, you with you, celebrating the birth of something unique? Are you comfortable with silence? What or who inspires you? Who do you respect the most? What does a spiritual life mean to you? Is there anybody home when you close the door? Who are you?

The observation of the movement of Yin and Yang through the seasons is one of the great teachings offered by life. It cost us nothing, yet is more valuable than almost anything else. My teacher, J. R. Worsley, said, *"If you can spend five minutes a day in Nature, you will learn far more how to practise this form of medicine than sitting here listening to me"*. (Clinical notes)

When we begin to relate to Nature as the one who supports and nourishes us, and as the one who guides and teaches us, we are once again in relationship. Nature is not something out there, Nature is a significant and vital part of my relationship with everything, including myself. The ancient Chinese show us a way to actually experience ourselves, one another, the planet and the stars as an integrated whole. Is it possible to harm the planet if we look at Nature in this way?

Through Nature as teacher and guide we re-establish a sense of connection that has been lost within and without us. All the wisdom cultures that we know revere Nature, connect through Nature. The sense of connection is vital for well-being.

"The force that through the green fuse drives the flower
Drives my green age; that blasts the root of trees
Is my destroyer.
And I am dumb to tell the crooked rose
My youth is bent by the same wintry fever"
(Dylan Thomas, 9)

"We know the sap which courses through the trees as we know the blood that courses through our veins. We are part of the earth and it is part of us. The perfumed flowers are our sisters. The bear, the deer, the great eagle, these are our brothers. The rocky crests, the dew in the meadow, the body heat of the pony, and man, all belong to the same family. The shining water that moves in the streams and rivers is not just water, but the blood of our ancestors... Each glossy reflection in the clear waters of the lakes tells of events and memories in the life of my people. The water's murmur is the voice of my father's father. The rivers are our brothers. They quench our thirst. They carry our canoes and feed our children. So you must give the rivers the kindness that you would give any brother."

(Selection from a letter by Chief Noah Sealth to Millard Fillmore, U.S. President, 1852)

The seasons are our teachers. Each season asks a question of us, relevant to every moment of our lives, but more accessible in a particular season because of its nature and function. Here are some of the questions of the seasons:

Winter	: Who am I? Why am I here?
Spring	: Where am I going? How do I express my uniqueness in the world?
Summer	: Am I living fully now?
Late Summer	: Do I belong? Where is the possibility of transformation?
Autumn	: What is precious about life? What do I no longer need?

Reality for the ancients was not relative. What was relative was our relationship to reality. Reality holds universal, eternal qualities such as tao, shen, yin yang, ming, the five elements, nature. Reality just is. Our raison d'etre is to ask - how do I relate to what is?

Chapter Eight
Suffering: The Experience of Suffering

What is suffering?

Xun Zi, a 3rd century BCE scholar, expresses it like this:
"No person who derides true principles in their mind
can fail to be led astray for undue attention to external objects.
No person who pays undue attention to external objects
can fail to feel anxiety in their mind.
No person whose behaviour departs from true principles
can fail to be endangered by external forces.
No person who is endangered by external forces
can fail to feel terror in their mind.
If the mind is filled with anxiety and terror,
then, though the mouth be crammed with delicious food,
it will not recognize the flavour;
though the ear listens to the music of bells and drums,
it will not recognize the sound;
though the eye light upon embroidered patterns,
it will not recognize their form;
and, though the body is clothed in warm, light garments
and rest upon fine, woven mats,
it will feel no ease."
(as qtd in Larre/Rochat de la Vallee, The Seven Emotions, 19)

One of the understandings of Buddhism is that although

life is suffering, if we can accept that life is suffering, then we no longer suffer. Suffering seems to be based on the refusal to accept what is. And yet, is not that refusal a part of being human - to want a "better" life for ourselves, our families, our people, our world? And does that not imply consciousness, dissatisfaction, hope, vision, ambition, and love? And are all these qualities aspects of the refusal to accept what is? Accordingly, could acceptance of what is be a form of resignation, where we are waiting for Godot, eyes downcast and dull, resigned to our fate?

The ancient Chinese saw it differently. Fate is different from destiny. Fate occurs when we are not aligned with our original nature, *Yuanshen*, therefore not aligned with our destiny, *Ming*, and therefore subject to external dynamics that scatter and fragment our being into scraps of material in the wind. In this scenario we have no centre, no place to stand, no place of self reflection, no sense of meaning. When we can align ourselves with our original nature and with the will of heaven, then our authentic self, our *Zhenqi*, is operative and generative within us and we have the opportunity and the means to become more of who we are, to fulfill ourselves, to live our destiny.

Childhood is often a matter of survival. As children we are subject to the power of adults, so we have to find what allows us to live with those around us. Survival often means abandoning ourselves, our *Yuanshen*, in order to function within our familial and social environment. This is the beginning of the inauthentic life. In addition we tend to want life to follow our desires, and we want to cherry-pick what experiences we have. When we are hooked on our desires, we no longer have perspective or understanding. Everything becomes more personal. As a result we are more vulnerable to circumstances outside our own bodies and outside our control. Once we develop a pattern that is increasingly based on attachment to external focus or reaction to stimuli, we are more susceptible to disorder in our lives and in our bodies. We have a less authentic life, a life of 'suffering'.

True principles are the principles of living according to the *Tao* which means placing the mystery at the centre of meaning and making it the catalyst for all that can be known. It means taking nature as one's guide, being trustfully patient, looking at oneself and everything else as a totality of relationships and life as a field of potential. Ignoring true principles results in us not being aligned with our true nature and our place in the cosmos. The inevitable result internally is anxiety and fear, even terror.

For the ancient Taoists anxiety and terror were not individual psychological states or pathologies to be 'treated' but existential realities, to which all people are subject when out of alignment. In this sense a 'psychological state' is primarily healthy feedback on our state of alignment, our positioning in relationship to existence. It, in itself, does not require attention. The modern, materialist approach to these psychological states tends to be a negative one. There is no recognition of the value of the experience. As a result, medication and therapy are used in an attempt to eliminate these states. The psychological state is a healthy feedback process, a flag waving to provoke attention. When we do not pay attention and destroy the flag, our organisms will resort to more powerful ways to get our attention, even to the point of killing us. Our organisms would rather choose material death than suffer living death. What requires attention is to look at how we are relating to circumstances, to look at the story we are telling ourselves about ourselves and our lives.

The dilemma of ignoring true principles goes hand in hand with the Taoist perception of the limitations. They are described in this way:

1. Belief in the limitation of an individual's power and potential to accomplish all things.
2. Belief in the limitation of an individual's power and potential to know all things.
3. Limitation of the ability to utilize the individual's power and potential by creating desire and attachment, giving rise to increasing discontentment.
4. Limitation of the utilization of an individual's power and potential by attachment to time-related changes (birth, growth, maturation, waning and death).
5. Limitation of the utilization of the individual's free will by creating fate, binding the individual to endless cycles of birth and death.

(Johnson. Chinese Medical Qigong Therapy, Vol.1, 114)

These limitations are really the restrictions we impose upon ourselves, usually based on a fear-driven desire to survive, and the closing of the window on spiritual experience and the meaning of our lives. The challenges of life, particularly when we are young, can result in us settling for less, becoming resigned, imbuing external objects and events with power over us, and identifying with our bodies rather than our spirits. The ignoring of true principles and the belief in the five limitations is the basis for suffering.

Suffering requires attachment. When I am attached, I am no longer free, because I am attached. I can only be free when I can come and go in relationship to everything. With attachment there is no "meeting place" between me and the something else before me. The essence of the Heart is an empathetic, compassionate relationship which is based on non-attachment. The ancient Chinese character for the heart shows a container with a seemingly empty space at its centre. The empty space is really a field of potential that can engage with every emotion without getting attached to it.

That said, as human beings living on earth we will always be attached. We cannot live beyond a few seconds without the oxygen that plants release into the atmosphere, or beyond a few days without water. We are attached, period. The issue for the Taoists is not attachment per se but our **relationship** to attachment. The great sage, Laozi, asks:

> *"Do you have the patience to wait*
> *till your mud settles and the water is clear?*
> *Can you remain unmoving*
> *till the right action arises by itself".*
> (Tao Te Ching, chapt.15)

Let us backtrack a little. Human beings are products of culture which is, in turn, reproduced through such discourses as gender based roles, external authority and laws, and subordination of the individual to the group through shaming, blaming and guilt, sacrifice and duty. These mechanisms keep the group intact and better able to deal with external dangers. Our evolutionary development is taking us further and further away from the collective into a process of individuation where we are emerging from within ourselves. Laozi says, *"If you want to know me, look inside your heart."*

As we let go of the tribe, we also let go of patterns of communication, structure and identity intrinsic to tribal culture. It is as if we have cast off from an island never to return and can rely only on ourselves. We have not yet created the ways as a culture to process and work with suffering. Carl G. Jung, the pioneering depth psychologist, suggested that we "do" consciousness through suffering when, in *Contributions to Analytical Psychology* he said, *"There is no coming to consciousness without pain"*.

Getting ill seems to be a significant way with which we start the exploration of consciousness, which will then help us not to stop suffering but to lift the burden of suffering. It is also the way we can let go of form, let go of control and plunge ourselves into the darkness within and below, the murky depths from which the new light of healing will come: from the realm of Xi Wang Mu, the Queen Mother of the West. I remember my own children, when young, collapsing into vomiting, diarrhoea, snot and phlegm, and, when they came through that process, they were changed. They seemed more conscious, more engaged. They had become more of who they were. They had developed into something new, and their maladies were the transformational mechanisms they used to do it.

Another insight into suffering comes from the *Neijing*. When asked by Huangdi, the Yellow Emperor, why people start declining when they reach the age of fifty, Qibo, his advisor, describes people living inappropriately, dissipation, recklessness and indulgence being the norm. *"It is not surprising"*, he says, *"that they look old at fifty."*

What Qibo is getting at is that the age fifty is a time when the body energy, the Jing, is declining. Before then, when the Jing was rising, people could ignore healthy ways of living because the Jing gave them the power to override those ways and live according to their wandering desires. In our fifties, as the Jing declines, it becomes increasingly difficult to pursue a lifestyle that is indulgent and unhealthy. The attempt to do so usually results in illness of one kind or another.

The positive spin on this process of rising and declining Jing is that rising Jing fuels our ambition while declining Jing fuels our wisdom. As Jing rises, we look at making our mark in the world in some way, our ambition is usually directed towards external priorities. As Jing declines, consciousness can develop since we are faced with a fundamental decline in our capacities, and can no longer sustain the habits of the past. Consciousness is an inner focus. So decline does not imply less. In terms of a fully developing human life it implies more. Whether we can grasp the meaning of this is another matter.

We know life produces suffering. How then do we ease the burden of suffering? The first issue is - has our suffering been witnessed? We need to have our suffering acknowledged and witnessed, no matter how seemingly trite or traumatic the cause. One of the traumas of many childhoods is the absence of a witness to suffering. If our suffering is not acknowledged, then it is as if our suffering, expressed through emotion, does not exist. As a result many suffer in silence and, consequently, have no relationship with some of their deepest, most vulnerable experiences. Fortunate are those whose childhood trials and tribulations have been enquired about, witnessed, validated. There is great danger in the absence of the witness. We can end up with an interior monologue about which we are seldom conscious, and, therefore, incapable of sharing. The lack of witness to our suffering, and therefore the difficulty in sharing or recounting the suffering, make our suffering a burden. And it is the burden of suffering that is actually the problem. In truth we can handle our suffering. We are designed to handle our suffering. We have the tools within us to engage authentically with suffering. What is impossible for us is experiencing suffering as a burden, because it is then life itself which is the burden.

How do we change our experience of suffering as a burden? How do we move to a place where we can have some breathing space and therefore some means for reflection, some means to feel and choose another way?

The witnessing of our suffering is the first step. It is of

major importance. First Nations people in Canada have met continuously after so many of them as children were forcibly removed from their homes and families by Canadian governments and put in what were euphemistically called 'residential schools' but which were actually concentration camps in which many children died. If they did not die, they were systematically physically, sexually and emotionally abused largely by the religious orders in charge of the camps. The people still come to meet in circles and talk about what they went through and what they are still going through, and to have that witnessed. Since the time of writing, Justice Murray Sinclair, head of the Canada Truth and Reconciliation Commission, and author of its report, described the experience of First Nations in Canada as "cultural genocide". Finally the suffering is being witnessed in the Canadian community as a whole. Witnessing the suffering is very important. In the Gospel according to Thomas, Jesus Christ says to Thomas, *"If you cannot bring out of you what is within you, it will destroy you"*.

After acknowledging our suffering, the next step is to reframe the suffering, tell our story of suffering in a different way, a way that liberates and potentiates us.

Chapter Nine
Suffering: Reframing the Suffering

"I am not what happened to me, I am what I choose to become."
(C. G. Jung, Memories, Dreams, Reflections)

In the previous chapter I talked about suffering and the burden of suffering and made reference to the stories we tell ourselves about ourselves. Rumi, the great Sufi mystic, writing one thousand years ago, has an interesting take on suffering:

"A craftsman pulled a reed from the reed-bed,
cut holes in it, and called it a human being.
Since then, it has been wailing a tender agony of parting,
never mentioning the skill that gave it life as a flute."
(Rumi, The Essential Rumi, 146)

Rumi and Jung are asking the question: which story do you want to tell - the story of loss and powerlessness or the story of creativity, of potential? They are both stories, but only one of them is potentiated, only one of them opens up to possibility, where the other is a dead end; only one of them travels close to reality where our response to reality is a creative act and unburdened freedom.

One of the five limitations identified by the Taoists is the limitation of self-definition through the history and biography of life, through the chronological experience of our finite experience of birth, growth, maturation, decline and death. Defining our lives through reference to past experience, through what has happened, is something we all do. It is challenging not to be shaped, for example, by trauma, or by the particular biography we have each had. Isn't that experience the means through which we define ourselves and shape our lives? When we look at the global conflicts of our own times, we see generations of people defining themselves through the past and its histories of conflict, revenge, and hatred. Karl Marx, the nineteenth century revolutionary, put it dramatically in *The Eighteenth Brumaire* when he said, "*The tradition of all the dead generations weighs like a nightmare on the brain of the living.*" (Marx, Karl. The 18th Brumaire of Louis Bonaparte). When I lived in Scotland, the common refrain was "aye been" - it's always been this way. Look at the slogan on the Quebec car plates "Je me reviens" - I remember. Telling the story of how the past limits our present is an ubiquitous human practice.

What privileges the past equally trenchantly is the collective, the group, the tribe. The group, in its structure and its culture, shapes itself through the collective experience of survival: the collective is more important than the individual, the traditions more important than the present, and external roles more important than inner experience. Today we seem to be in transition from a group life shaped by external references (for example, role, gender, race, nation, law, materialism, consumerism, fate) to a life shaped by inner references (for example, health, fulfillment, relationship, contribution, self realization, purpose, meaning, destiny).

To the extent that we can free ourselves from the domination of the past, then we free ourselves from the burden of suffering caused by such domination. In addition to roles and traditions, the past manifests in us as the experience in our bodies of something that is in us but not of us: what is described by Chang Po-Tuan, the 11th century Taoist adept and author of the great classic, *Understanding Reality*, as "acquired conditioning". Chang Po-tuan says:

> *"Real knowledge is all real,*
> *But it needs to be espoused by conscious knowledge.*
> *Refining away acquired conditioning,*
> *The two become one whole."*

"Real knowledge" is existence itself. When we look at a daffodil, we see knowledge organized at the level of existence, of being. Being and consciousness are so integrated in the daffodil, we are not aware of it. The daffodil 'knows' what to do in order to grow and become itself. As far as we know, it does not wish to become a tulip or feel downcast that its colour is paler than another daffodil's. It is complete in itself, so complete that consciousness and existence are one and the same thing. It is the huge influence of acquired conditioning in all its forms that presents the greatest challenge to the "refining away" of which Chang Po-Tuan speaks. I am emphasizing collective conditioning as a major influence in our time simply because we are moving beyond it. We are birthing something new. Wisdom cultures have great teachings for us. At the same time wisdom manifesting through predefined roles does not fit well with our modern way. Taking up a culturally predetermined role was part of the collective past experience, but we are individuating beyond the ability of roles to contain us. If wisdom relates to awakening, consciousness, then where in the absence of adequate roles do we "do" consciousness in our times? As I mentioned in the section on suffering, we do it, at least initially, through the body.

Our bodies, as transformational wisdom embodied and organized at the level of the material, will throw out signs and signals to alert us to this issue, whether they be physical ailments, mental and emotional crises, spiritual challenges. In other words, and as a seeming paradox, our pathologies are intentional signals sent by our bodies to encourage us to develop a new consciousness within. Remember the words of Jesus Christ in The Gospel of Thomas:

> *"If you bring forth what is inside you,*
> *what you bring forth will save you.*
> *If you do not bring forth what is inside you,*
> *what you do not bring forth will destroy you."*

So the issue is how do we bring forth what is inside us? Acknowledging and having our suffering witnessed is a start. Reframing our experience of suffering is a further step. When we carry our suffering as a burden, it is the same as carrying our life as a burden. A patient of mine was referred to me by a friend and was described as having had a nervous breakdown. Unable even to put a plug in a socket, she seemed to have collapsed. She told me a story of enslavement to a man, for whom she was used only as a servant. Eventually she left. Having left, she collapsed and fell into the arms of my friend who gave her a bed, food, and love. I felt that she had not had a nervous breakdown but a nervous breakout, a nervous break-in, that her response was completely healthy, and, given all she had been through, it was natural and healthy that she would be healing deep within herself, at the level of the spirit, with no room to pay attention to more practical functions such as making a cup of tea. Plus, she had not gone to a doctor who would probably have given her an anti-depressant, but to a friend who would take her in and enfold her in unconditional, non-judgmental love. Everything she had done was in fact completely healthy. This alternative way of looking at the situation matched her real sense of herself, giving her a place to stand and acknowledge the truth of the matter. She was immediately more relaxed, more present, more empowered and therefore more hopeful about how to live after this terrible abuse.

Every impulse is inherently life-affirming within us. I call this the virtue. If we frame an experience as bad, wrong, unhealthy, we may well miss the point. The focus on behaviour is a focus that freeze-frames a situation unproductively and is often accompanied by attitudes of guilt, shame, humiliation and condemnation which result in a separation from the self and from others - we end up in a dead-end street with nowhere to go. The reframing of 'pathology' can open up choices connected to the truth of the matter. As a result we will be more energized, more empowered, more creative in relationship to ourselves.

Can we get behind the behaviour and look at the healthy impulse, the virtue, instead? Take the example of cigarette smoking. Cigarette smoking is bad for your health. Even cigarette packets state it! But people still smoke. Why? According to Health Canada half of daily smokers have a nicotine dependency. Assuming 50% of smokers do not have a nicotine dependency, why do they still smoke? Cigarette smoking includes two aspects - inhaling the heated smoke of the tobacco and breathing more deeply when inhaling. A smoker takes in heat and breathes more deeply. Heat is warmth is love. If there is not enough inner warmth in my life and a loving relationship with myself and others is challenging; if the thermostatic function in my body is not working very well and I cannot regulate temperature appropriately within my body; if I have no experience of divine love within my heart so that in my spirit I am like a man in a snowstorm far from the warming fire of home, then smoking cigarettes could be appealing.

As a boy I saw a cinema ad where a man is standing on a bridge over the river Thames in the dead of night. As he lights a cigarette, the slogan crosses the screen and reads, "You're never alone with a Strand". In this ad a cigarette is a friend or at least a means to overcome the undesired feeling of loneliness. In addition, when we draw deeply on a cigarette, we actually cause the blood vessels to dilate, causing more blood and oxygen to flow through the vessels, and causing the body to relax to some extent.

Every impulse is inherently good even though the

paths we choose to materialize that impulse are not necessarily helpful, stemming as they do from acquired conditioning. If we mainly look at inauthentic or harmful behaviour, it is very difficult to accomplish anything since it is almost impossible to stand in the negative. We have to get to the virtue behind the negative to get a true sense of ourselves and to have somewhere to stand vis-a-vis our behaviour. If we look beyond the smoking behaviour, the symptom, to what is actually behind it, we discover a need for more warmth in the body, mind and spirit, and for more relaxation. Once we reframe in this way, we open up the experience from being 'bad' behaviour, a negative snapshot frozen in time, to a means of understanding that what we really need is warmth, love, relaxation.

It is the same with overeating. If we are overeating, eating for comfort, taking nightly raids into the fridge, consuming all things sweet, it is not 'bad' or unhealthy behaviour. We are doing it because we do not feel nourished by our lives, by existence itself. Food is a metaphor and a real expression of nourishment. Nourishment is to do with the Mother within us, since it is from the Mother that we are nourished. We use the expression Mother Earth to indicate that. When we comfort eat, when we eat sweet, we want to fill ourselves up, just like a baby at the mother's breast. When we feel full, although we may feel better, in reality we have only stuffed down emotions that make us feel uncomfortable, orphaned and alone. Those emotions, if explored, can offer direction towards a more nourishing life, bring us closer to the Mother within us who is only too ready and willing to support us. We can scan our lives and look at what truly nourishes us and what does not. Behaviour is a part of an intelligent feed-back loop operating through our bodies. Constructed through our conditioning it is the beginning point of self-discovery, of consciousness. It points to the absolute truth of the spirit, of the soul.

Cancer needs a major reframe to release it from the fear of death it triggers within us. The association of cancer and death is, in my view, more dangerous than the cancer itself. Cancer has been portrayed as an aggressor. We hear about 'the war against cancer', about 'cancer victims'. According to the Public Health Agency of Canada cancer is the leading cause of death. A similar perspective is found in the U.S. and the U.K. Almost 50% of the UK population is expected to develop cancer. Liver, kidney and thyroid cancers are significantly rising and are strongly linked to lifestyle choices. (See Cancer Research UK, U.S. National Cancer Institute).

So what is cancer? Cancerous cells are cells that have forgotten their purpose, that is, they have forgotten what they are supposed to do and where they are supposed to go. They hang around and multiply. I compare them to bored teenagers who gather on street corners in increasing numbers, eventually spilling over into the road and causing major interruption of traffic flow. Some then migrate to other street corners and do the same thing there. The result - chaos. So, at the most fundamental level of existence, the cell, we have been losing the plot.

It is a mistake to assume that cancer is one more disease alongside others. In previous times disease was more fragmented - disease of organs, of bones, of blood, of the nervous system.

With cancer, the centre stage is occupied by the cell itself - the building block of life. We are now dealing with the whole of ourselves, not a part. All pathologies are a wake-up call. With disease, illness, pain, we no longer take anything for granted, are more grounded, start to get our priorities sorted out. The problem is, if our organisms do not see real progress in our consciousness, they will manifest stronger and stronger symptoms to get our attention, hence the emergence of cancer.

It is no accident that cancer emerges alongside other 'total' experiences such as climate change, global economic crises, ecological catastrophes, genocidal wars. We are now engaged in total experiences where everything is related, everything connected. People and nature, people and people, the inner and the outer, all are being experienced by more and more people as one. A teenager of the Coast Salish peoples of Vancouver Island once said to me, "Between us all we have a blanket. When you pull your corner, I feel it." We are now more closely connected than ever before through the worldwide web. Everything is to do with relationship. Out of the necessity of relationship comes greater communication, greater felt connection, greater collectively shared insights. The world now experiences itself more as one world, and cancer offers the often undesired opportunity to experience ourselves as one whole being, where everything affects everything else, where we cannot separate diet from relationship, work from spirituality. Everything is impacting everything else, because everything "is" everything else. We can more easily replace the illusion of the separate, the fragmented, the partial with the realization that we are fundamentally one.

Whether we have or have not developed cancer in our own bodies, its emergence as a major force in our collective health is affecting us all in some way. It is encouraging us to experience ourselves as no longer fragmented, with no split of body, mind and spirit, with no split of inner and outer life. Running through all experience is a golden thread. That golden thread is us. Laozi says, "*She who is centred in the Tao... perceives the universal harmony, even amid great pain, because she has found peace in her heart*". (Tao Te Ching, chapt. 35). We are being encouraged to remember, that is to re-member, to bring all the members of our self together again as one being. The contemplation and experience of cancer helps us drop our attachment to externals and reorganize our priorities around a truer, more authentic self.

Perhaps the most fundamental reframing that is needed are the stories we tell ourselves about ourselves. These stories are shaped by the way we relate to our experience. The dominant group/subordinate individual pattern is primarily influenced by outside factors such as other people's opinions, especially those whom we hold dear, such as friends and members of our family, and pre-existing beliefs and values. The subordination of the individual to the collective tends to encourage ways such as self-sacrifice and martyrdom, and attitudes such as guilt, shame and blame.

These 'outside' stories are the experiences that are in us but not of us. The stories we learn are so embedded, that we may not even be aware that they are stories. The way we can tell if a story is 'in us but not of us' is whether we feel we are enriched by the stories we tell of our lives. If we have a tragic tale to tell, for example, a story that we were damaged as a child by X and it has determined our whole life, then the question we need to ask is, how does this story serve us? Do we feel lighter, brighter, richer, stronger, more? Or do we feel darker, narrower, heavier, poorer, weaker, less? If we feel the latter, then we are experiencing something in us that is not of us. We have not found the treasure within, that is, ourselves. Therefore we are not living in reality.

'Outside' stories are essentially stories of survival: survival from our families, our childhoods, from societal pressures and demands. They do not come from inner-generated forces, but from reaction to outer-generated forces. Embodied reaction to outer-generated forces is anchored in us through our 'acquired spirit', our *shenzhi*, which develops in us through our engagement with life. If we fail to connect with our inner-generated forces, our *yuanshen*, we run the risk that our 'acquired spirit', which wants stability and wishes to secure physical, mental and emotional survival, will become resistant to inner transformation, thus resulting in what the Taoists call 'acquired conditioning' - the physical, mental, emotional and spiritual dynamics that are in us, but not of us.

A prerequisite for the reframing of our suffering is the understanding of our 'acquired conditioning'. 'Acquired conditioning' is best approached from the perspective of choice. When we can acknowledge the choices we made in order to survive, we start to move beyond 'acquired conditioning'. Through the acknowledgement of choice, we begin to empower and reconnect with our *Yuanshen*.

Another take on the stories we tell and on the reframing of suffering is offered, once again, by Rumi:

> *"When grapes turn to wine,*
> *they long for our ability to change.*
> *When stars wheel*
> *around the North Pole,*
> *they are longing for our growing consciousness.*
> *Wine got drunk in us,*
> *not the other way.*
> *The body developed out of us, not we from it.*
> *We are bees,*
> *and our body is a honeycomb.*
> *We made the body,*
> *cell by cell we made it."*
> (Rumi, as qtd. in The Enlightened Heart, 53)

For Rumi existence is a creative act: *"the body developed out of us, not we from it"*. We are both the conch shell calling us to transform, and the transformation itself. He would have felt at home with the Taoists. The quotation from Rumi asserts that our material form results from our energetic engagement with life, not the other way around. We are fields of potential that materialize matter, that materialize our bodies, not biomechanical building blocks 'accidentally' producing consciousness. Sages like Rumi, a thousand years in the past, become significant to us today, because they are speaking about reality in ways that meet us in our evolving modern-day consciousness.

Increasingly, we are being called to go beyond 'acquired conditioning' and move towards truth, authenticity, reality. This is what Goethe meant when he said, *"Die and become"*. We need to reframe our stories according to destiny, that is, through our inner-generated choices; not according to fate, that is, where consciousness is a meaningless by-product of a pre-existing bio-mechanical truth.

Laozi has a plan to break out of the 'acquired conditioning', out of the disconnected *Shenzhi*, and accomplish the move towards *Yuanshen* :

"I have just three things to teach:
simplicity, patience, compassion.
These three are your greatest treasures.
Simple in actions and in thoughts,
you return to the source of being.
Patient with both friends and enemies,
you accord with the way things are.
Compassionate towards yourself,
you reconcile all beings in the world."
(Tao Te Ching, chapt. 67)

Laozi's 'source of being' is the *Yuanshen*, but also even further and deeper than that, back to the great Tao that *'nourishes infinite worlds'*. Simplicity eliminates confusion, creates a clear field of potential. Patience creates space and gives us the means to better relate and to accept life as it comes without personalizing everything into a melodrama with ourselves at centre stage. Compassion starts inside creating inner warmth, and resonates from within our souls to existence everywhere. Through the soul, which is part of my 'infinite' nature, I can connect even with a pebble on a beach in Bali.

So who are we? What is truly real about us? The Taoists say that what is truly real is our original nature to which we have to return, our *Yuanshen*. It is through our original nature that we can be in relationship to the unknowable and mysterious field of potential at the core of life. Reframing our suffering and creating new, energetically-generative and dynamic stories about the unfolding of our lives is part of the process of returning to our original nature, and, therefore, reality.

A second way to sense our original nature is by what inspires us. Inspiration can come from other people, dead, alive, fictional, mythical; from artefacts; from art, literature and music; from circumstances and events; from our own imaginations. Inspiration can come from anywhere. Where there is inspiration, there is the soul singing. It is worth looking at the Lung at this point. In classical Chinese medicine the ancients looked at function rather than organs. So when they talked about the Lung, they meant far more than the organ. They saw the organ as a material expression of an energetic function and an energetic relationship. The Lung is described as the Official who Receives Pure Qi from the Heavens. The Lung takes in the truth of ourselves, the absolute pure essence of who we really are. It is characterized by inspiration; on the physical level the breath, but at a deeper level, the essence of self. Saint Francis of Assisi says, *"What you are looking for is what is looking."* So the 'Lung", as the expression of received truth, has to be in every part of us, body, mind and spirit. Inspiration takes us to our core.

After reframing and inspiration we can develop practices that can strengthen wisdom within us at the cellular level - embodied wisdom. Embodied wisdom or embodied consciousness is the core structural change that the Taoists believed possible through the many exoteric and esoteric practices they undertook. Consciousness has to occur at the cellular level. If not, it becomes a floating state, potentially leaving us more ungrounded than ever before. It can produce a state of happiness while our lives crumble around us. We need to earth consciousness in our bodies, we need to earth Heaven. And that is what the Taoists were all about.

The practice of what is called qigong, for example, is based on the attention to the breath descending into the area of the kidneys. Why? Because the inspiration of the Lungs is momentary. It needs something else to anchor it in the body. The Kidney energy - that which causes life to endure beyond the present moment - is the fundamental bridge between the breath and the body, and anchors the qi breath in the body. When the Kidneys are weak, therefore, the qi of the breath is not anchored in the body, and floats up into the area of the Lungs, gets stuck there, and causes all kinds of illnesses related to the Lung such as asthma, pneumonia, allergies, colds and flus, bronchial issues.

Chapter Ten
The Challenge to Reframing the Suffering

The challenge to reframing our suffering comes from some of the experiences and developments I have mentioned earlier: acquired conditioning, attachment, the five limitations, the strategies for surviving childhood, the lack of alignment with true principles, the predominantly yang culture of the modern world, the focus on behaviour and symptoms rather than the virtue behind them.

Another significant challenge to reframing is the experience of transformation itself. The commitment to transformation (living our own lives, living with integrity, moving beyond conditional love (which isn't love at all), placing a priority on inner values, spiritual practice) creates a conflict between our soul's need to sing and our acquired conditioning's need to suppress vitality. This process results in awareness, vulnerability, gratitude, appreciation, humility, spontaneity, deeper loving as well as self doubt, fear, uncertainty, ambiguity, physical ailments, irrationality, loneliness, desperation, tears and more tears, awkwardness, incoherence. In the midst of the process of transformation there are no straight lines anymore, no recognizable landmarks, no comfort of the familiar.

Everybody knows, deep down inside, that we will be seriously challenged by our rebirthing, our alchemical process of transformation. The First Nations in Canada say that, sooner or later, you come to the void, the abyss, and you have to leap. I watched a mother moose cross a swift-flowing river and then wait for the young bull moose to follow. All day he bellowed as he looked at her on the other side of the river. All day she waited for him. He was never alone or abandoned. Finally, as dusk came, he took the plunge. He leaped into the void. He crossed the river. He was reborn as Moose.

The First Nations, and other wisdom cultures, had and have a structure of support for the journey through the void. In modern-day Western culture we are faced with creating those structures within and between ourselves. Our teachers and gurus are within, our sacred books are within. We are charting a different way, cultivating the resources and the support we need to do this different way. When the disabling or challenging experiences of the transformational journey occur, we often fail to understand that they are precisely that. Instead we mistake them as negativities that scare and confuse us. Being at depth within ourselves is often uncomfortable because in the past our experience of depth has been coupled with negativity, with crisis, with pain. When the transformation is underway within us, we find we cannot stop it. We cannot stop the flow of tears, the movement away from recognizable form. We have moved beyond the point of no return. Combined with depth experienced as negativity, we can feel really scared and helpless.

What a blessing if, faced with a particular challenge, an elder could say to you, "Oh, you are going through 3a. You need to do this or that, and then you will get to 3b, where you will probably experience this or that. Go and see so-and-so when this happens". In our world it is not going to work that way. When I witness my patients going through this journey, I share with them that these seemingly negative experiences are in fact the experience of transformation that with patience, recognition and practices that support the embodiment of wisdom can be successfully bridged to enable the birth of something new, the true self, *Yuanshen*.

Yes, it is a big challenge. But actually it's the only game in town. Once you begin your quest, there is no turning back. Once you step on the train, you discover there never was an 'off the train', it was an illusion that supported a fragmented, disconnected life. People with cancer are brought to the realization that faces us all, that we will die. We have many ways to distance ourselves from this inevitability, and many of us conduct our lives as if we will live forever. People with cancer are brought to the meeting place with mortality and, for the most part, initially struggle with that meeting. Initially there is the profound terror, especially if they wish to live. And then it becomes a reflection on, and planning of, supportive priorities - what can I do to overcome the cancer? They become more conscious and begin to question their lifestyle. Diet, exercise, relationship, spirituality - all come into the mix. Eventually the focus moves from cancer to a more existential question - how do I live more fully now? (A question that I came across when visiting the Quest Center for Integrative Health in Portland, Oregon). This is the question behind all the ancient Taoist work.

The process through which the Taoists and some of the

people with cancer go is a process of alchemical transformation, letting go of form in the shape of past attachments and patterns that do not support them anymore, releasing the desire to control, trusting their own intuition and instincts, and allowing something else, something new to emerge, that is, the mystery of themselves, *Yuanshen*.

The challenges to reframing the suffering are challenges because they are there to help develop our capacity to engage with transformation. No training is easy when it goes beyond talking. And this is as much a training as a Zen Buddhist life in a monastery is a training. It is inner training, and we are engaged in this inner training in the mundane outer life. We have been invited to do what I call the monastery in the marketplace. This is hinted at by Huang Yuan-ch'i in his 13th century C.E. Annals of the Hall of Blissful Development, (The Taoist I Ching):

"People are happy when there is quiet and vexed when there is commotion. Don't they realize that since their energy has already been stirred by the clamour of people's voices and the involvements and disturbances of people and affairs, rather than use this power to be annoyed at the commotion, it is better to use this power to cultivate stability. An ancient said, when people are in the midst of disturbance, this is a good time to apply effort to keep independence, stay comprehensively alert in the immediate present, and that suddenly an awakening will open up an experience in the midst of it all that is millions of times better than that of quiet sitting. Whenever you encounter people making a commotion, whether it concerns you or not, use it to polish and strength-

en yourself, like gold being refined over and over until it no longer changes colour. If you gain power in this, it is much better than one drawn-out practice in quietude." (Taoist I Ching, 13)

The collision of soul and acquired conditioning invites us to cultivate many supports for getting through the process. We each have to find what works for us. The support has to be strong enough to help overcome the conditioning at the level of the cells in our bodies. Part of the Taoist approach was to cultivate activities which could help do that. The strengthening of embodied wisdom is the anticipated result of of those activities, of that intention. Consciousness joining with existence, with what is, is the Taoist goal. Not only does this empower us, it also allows us to see that suffering is no longer a burden, because suffering has been put into the alchemical mix of transformation.

Eternal Tao doesn't do anything, yet it leaves nothing undone.
If you abide by it, everything in existence will transform itself.
When, in the process of self-transformation,
desires are aroused, calm them with nameless simplicity.
When desires are dissolved in the primal presence,
peace and harmony naturally occur, and the world orders itself.
(Tao Te Ching, chapt. 37)

Chapter Eleven
The Meeting Place

"The place where the this and the that
are not opposed to each other
is called 'the pivot of the tao'
When we find this pivot, we find ourselves
at the centre of the circle,
and here we sit, serene,
while Yes and No keep chasing each other
around the circumference, endlessly."
(Zhuangzi, chapt. 6, trans. Mitchell, The Second Book of the Tao)

"In the pursuit of knowledge,
every day something is added.
In the practice of the Tao
every day something is dropped.
Less and less do you need to force things,
until finally you arrive at non-action.
When nothing is done,
nothing is left undone.
Take the entire world as nothing.
Make the least effort
and the world escapes you"
(Tao Te Ching, chapt. 48, Mitchell, Addiss and Lombardo)

"When nothing is done, nothing is left undone", says

Laozi. What does this mean? Laozi is telling us that our agendas usually interfere with our capacity to be real. As a result, actions, thoughts, feelings occur, but they have no true meaning or value, no resonance with innermost nature, our *Yuanshen*. When we let go of our agendas, our desires and fears, then movement, thought and feeling naturally arise in a way that is appropriate and in accord with our *Yuanshen*, with both who we really are and with reality.

How does this work? A fundamental aspect of Taoist understanding of reality is that everything that we need is already there; that we are designed with the divine wisdom written into our blood, our cells, our minds and spirits. This is our original nature, *Yuanshen*, our soul life, that provides the connection with the *Shen*, and infuses our lives with meaning. In response to acquired conditioning, our purpose is to engage in a process that frees us to re-experience *Yuanshen*, to know and potentiate it in our individual lives.

For the ancient Chinese the centre of ourselves is the *Wu*, the empty, unknowable mystery at the core of being. *Wu* is the potential within us that is in accordance with our *Yuanshen*. Through this potential, guidance, inspiration, insight, knowledge, understanding and compassion, all come into being. The human expression of *Wu* is the field of potential and organization of life that is the Heart. *Wu* and Heart are two sides of the same coin, the coin of life.

The notion of *Wu* is strange for us to grasp. And yet we have all experienced it. That is the *Wu* where, without being forced, the energy has a life of its own, and will always align it-self with the truth, with the highest purpose of who we are and what we are about. This is how Master Zhuang talks about it:

Lord Wen-hui's cook, Ting, was cutting up an ox. With every touch of his hand, every heave of his shoulder, every step of his foot, every thrust of his knee, he sliced with his zinging knife, everything was in perfect resonance...

"Wonderful!" said Lord Wen-hui. "What incredible skill!"

Ting stopped, laid down his knife and said, *"I follow the Tao, which goes beyond skill. When I first began cutting up oxen, all I could see was the ox itself. After three years I no longer saw the whole ox. And now - now I work with my inner. Inner follows its own path. I go along with the natural structure, my knife finds its own way through the hidden openings, never touching ligament or bone. A good cook changes his knife once a year - he cuts. An ordinary cook changes his knife every month - he hacks. I've had this knife nineteen years, it has cut up thousands of oxen and is still as sharp as when I first got it. Between the joints there are spaces. My knife has no thickness and slides into those spaces with room to spare. When I come to a difficulty, I pay close atten-tion, slow down and let the knife, with the slightest of movements, find its own way; then, all of a sudden, the whole thing falls apart like a clod of earth crumbling to the ground. I stand there awhile enjoying the moment fully. Then I clean my knife and put it away."*

"Brilliant!', cried the Lord. *"From my cook I have learned the secret of life."* (Zhuangzi, Inner Chapters, chapt.3)

The experience of the *Tao* that Ting knows comes from his

understanding of *Wu*. *Wu* and Heart working together through Ting is implied in his comment, *"I work with my inner. Inner follows its own path"*. Implicit in Zhuangzi's story is the lack of effort required. Effort only becomes effort when will and activity are not aligned with the *Tao*.

Understanding *Wu* is a felt experience, a knowing that is intrinsic to human life. It is not a philosophical concept, but an embodied gift given us to enable us to experience our relationship with ourselves, with one another, with nature and the cosmos, all in one moment, continuously, endlessly, forever. It is the means for us to know without knowing, what the ancients called *wuwei*. It is at the core of all spiritual experience, the inner reality of ourselves. Zhuangzi tells it brilliantly in his story about P'ien, the wheelwright:

> *Duke Huan was in his hall reading a book. P'ien, the wheelwright, was working on a wheel in the yard below. Then he laid down his tools, walked into the hall and asked Duke Huan,*
> *"May I ask, Your Grace, what you are reading?"*
> *"I am reading the words of the sages", said the Duke.*
> *"Are the sages still alive?"*
> *"No, they died a long time ago."*
> *"So you're reading the dregs they left behind."*
> *"How dare you, a wheelwright, make such a comment on what I, a Duke, am reading!", shouted Duke Huan. "Explain yourself, or else you die!"*
> *"Thank you, your Grace, I will", said P'ien. "When I'm working on a wheel, and I tap the chisel too softly, it slides over the wood. If I hit it too hard, it gets wedged in the wood. When*

the force is neither too soft, nor too hard, I know it in my hands, I know it in me. It's something I know but can't put into words. I can't teach it to my son, and he can't learn it from me. After seventy years as a wheelwright, I won't be able to pass it on to anybody. When the old sages died, they took their knowing with them. That's why I described your book as the dregs."
(Zhuangzi, chapt. 13)

In one fell swoop Zhuangzi has united all of life, the mundane (the wheel) and the celestial (the sages), and shown the golden thread that links them, Wuwei, knowing without knowing. He takes it even further:

The purpose of a fish trap is to catch fish,
and when the fish are caught, the trap is forgotten.
The purpose of a rabbit snare is to catch rabbits.
When the rabbits are caught, the snare is forgotten.
The purpose of words is to convey meaning.
When meaning is grasped, the words are forgotten.
Where can I meet a man who has forgotten words?
He is the one I would like to talk to.
(Zhuangzi, chapt. 26)

Zhuangzi is talking about *Wuwei*. *"Where can I meet a man who has forgotten words?"* Knowing without knowing occurs when the knowing is embodied, consciousness has translated into the body and the innermost part of ourselves, and head knowledge is no longer needed. In the quotation above, "words" represent living in the head, "forgotten" means consciousness integrated into the body.

We have all experienced this in the most mundane of ways - driving a car. Learning to drive, we are conscious of everything: the gears, the steering wheel, the rear view mirror, the indicators, the speed, the road lane, etc. We can be so overwhelmed by it all that our body senses cannot cope and we stall the car, make some mistake in some way. It is as if our consciousness is not in our bodies at this point, but outside our bodies. Over time consciousness is gradually absorbed into the body, so that the hands and feet know what to do, the eyes know what to do. After a while driving almost seems automatic. It isn't automatic - it is where consciousness and body memory are both present in reality. Driving is an example of embodied consciousness where the continual meeting of consciousness and body results in a transformed process of consciousness. We know without knowing.

THE MEETING PLACE

What is the fundamental process that can support the relationship to *Wu*, to the experience of *Wuwei*? It is through what I call the Meeting Place. The Meeting Place is the golden thread running through Tao and all the qualities of ancient Chinese reality, through the reframing of suffering, and through our own lives. It is the means par excellence whereby we, in the 21st century, can engage with the essence and wisdom not only of the Taoists but also with the essence and wisdom of ourselves.

When we go to the Meeting Place there is no agenda other than to go to the Meeting Place. We are not trying to do anything, we are not trying to make something happen, we are not leading or following, we have no expectation, no hope, no fear, no disappointment. We are not focused on outcome, only on process, that is, the Meeting Place. The Meeting Place focusses on an agenda-less relationship with everything and everyone, but particularly with ourselves. In the meeting place we are truly aligned with ourselves. It creates the basis for appropriate response, an enriched and meaningful life, and the opportunity to contribute value to our own life, the life of our families and the life of our communities.

Byron Katie, who has initiated a particularly interesting form of self-enquiry, understands the value of the Meeting Place. In her book, *A Thousand Names for Joy*, she says, *"I don't let go of my thoughts. I meet them with understanding. Then **they** let go of me."*
(Katie, A Thousand Names for Joy, xiv)

The Meeting Place is all about accessing what Zhuangzi describes as *"the force that guided their steps"* (when referring to the ancient sages) as opposed to the end product, the form, the outcome, the symptom. The Meeting Place places the emphasis on relationship. Not on me, not on you, not on it. It engages with the place in-between. For the Taoists everything is about relationship. Their fundamental question is about how to relate to what is. And isn't that our issue as well? Whether we look into our personal worlds, our social, cultural, political and spiritual worlds, aren't we struggling with the question of relationship?

J. R. Worsley, my teacher, talked about the role of the acupuncturist as Mother Nature's assistant. Mother Nature speaks through the patient in ways that reveal what she wishes the acupuncturist to do. The acupuncturist's purpose is simply to pay attention to what she is wishing, and to do it." In order to receive from Mother Nature the acupuncturist has to show up in the Meeting Place. The whole of the training in the classical acupuncture work was to turn up in the Meeting Place.

This was most vividly expressed in Dr. Worsley's notion of "rapport". If you cannot establish rapport with patients, they will not open themselves to you. Rapport is the practice of going to the meeting place with someone. In the College of Traditional Acupuncture UK classroom we would practise all kinds of ways of exploring rapport. It could be in the manner of speech, it could be in the words used, it could be in the positioning of one's body in relation to the patient. Everything was used. Developing rapport was the most significant skill and most potent force in the classical work advocated by J. R. Worsley. When rapport was established, *Wu/Heart* was operative: the patient opened up, the treatments were potentiated and destiny could unfold more fully. I saw fellow students pass all their written examinations but be failed because of their inability to develop rapport.

The Meeting Place is not only the place where rapport take us. It is the most powerful place for healing and transformation. Why is that? In the Meeting Place there is no form. It only comes into being at the moment that we go there. It is not like dense material such as muscle, bone, tissue. It is the part of us that is in between. It is the space between material things. Where there is no form, there is no limit. Where there is no limit, there is maximum power, transformational healing power.

Just imagine if we could see inside our living body as it engaged with life. We would see all the material reality, the bones, the organs, the blood, the musculature, but we would also see something approximating sparkling light, glistening and shining, coursing, opening, closing, expanding, contracting, playing within and between everything. When somebody is truly alive, don't we describe them as shining, as if light is emitting from them? Or the look in their eyes as sparkling and dancing, brightening our world? The very first point of the Bladder meridian is called Eyes Bright or Eyes Clear. The meaning is that once you start seeing with the eye of your spirit, you will see things you never dreamed existed. Instead of merely looking, you will be seeing. These sparkling, shining forces are both the Meeting Place and what we engage with in the Meeting Place, in ourselves and in the other, namely Tao.

The Meeting Place is the no-thing in the some-thing. It is the formless place within the form. It is the confirmation that we are not essentially material beings. The material is the way we can access the immaterial, the formless, the no-thing. Everything that could be available to us is available when we go to the Meeting Place. As Laozi puts it in chapter 11 of the *Tao Te Ching*: "*We work with being, but it is non-being that we use*".

When we go in with agendas, expectations, attachments, we

are trying to impose form on the formless, trying to limit that which is without limitation. As the ancients cryptically commented, "You cannot help God".

Dr. Worsley once said to a group of us:
"Who you think you are is a very small part of who you are. It is the part of yourself with which you are most comfortable. You will need to stretch yourself beyond anything you currently imagine, because you will have to embrace everybody who enters your clinic. If you cannot embrace everybody, they will not come to you for treatment." (clinical notes).

The only way to embrace everybody, is to meet them. The larger part of me, my soul, or more accurately the unknown mystery of myself, what the Taoists called 'the shining mind', is the part that does all the work, that is clued into the divine programme, that can help me with every choice, every thought, every action. It is the part of me that operates within the Meeting Place. The conscious part of me is only the assistant that leads me to meet the larger part of me, the meeting of which produces the necessary action. My conscious mind enables me to put the plug in the socket, but the juice that flows through the cable has its own source. In the clinical training the understanding was that, when rapport was established, when you were in the Meeting Place, that the healing process became more accessible, more potent, that a clear clean field of potential had literally opened up, like a flower opening, like an angel smiling.

Fritz Smith, the discoverer and pioneer of Zero Balancing, a bodywork exploring the relationship of energy and structure, talks about the Meeting Place as the Zero Balance. The Zero Balance is the place in the body where, if you can hold the person, right there, in the body, without judgment or comparison, they will rise to their highest benefit. In other words it is the art of 'doing' nothing, doing the no-thing in the some-thing, going to the Meeting Place. This is the essence of Tao.

The healing power that is released through going to the Meeting Place involves a potentiation of all that is transformative within us - transformative, that is, in the direction of who we really are. This is the greatest power we have, being who we are. The power from our being, from our existence, is far greater than the limited powers of disease, of torment and anguish, of despair, or even conscious effort.

In Western culture we put a strong emphasis on what we can consciously do, on intention, on belief, on positive thought, on knowledge. None of this is wrong; creative action and intention are essential for life to be lived. Yet without the receptive, yielding force of mystery and unknowing within us, there is no balance. The conscious action can have greater value, more truth, when it places the mystery at the centre of life, and faces that mystery. Conscious action gets us to the Meeting Place. Then it has to back off and allow the mystery its free rein to reveal, to surprise, to offer the unexpected gift, to take us always beyond whatever and wherever we thought we were at that moment. The purpose of consciousness is to create and hold a space in which life, the mystery, the reality, the truth, destiny can sort itself out. In ch.48 of the Tao Te Ching it says, *"True mastery can be gained by letting things go their own way"*.

Gary Lineker, a famous English footballer turned sports broadcaster, who scored many goals in his playing career, was once asked the secret of his success. He answered, "My job was to turn up in the eighteen yard box (an area 108ft wide and 54ft long surrounding the opposition's goal). Nine times out of ten a ball never came, but the tenth time it did and I kicked it in the net (between the opposition's goalposts)." In other words he understood that his job was to go to the Meeting Place. In a similar vein my teacher, J. R. Worsley, said, *"You are first a resource to people, and secondly you are an acupuncturist"* (clinical notes). In this context *"acupuncturist"* means predefined agenda, *"resource"* means going to the Meeting Place.

Gary Neville, another footballer turned sports pundit, commenting on one of the competing teams in a football match, described the cause of their poor play as their attempt to "force" the game. In other words they were not playing within the Meeting Place, but out of fear or frustration and therefore not aligned with themselves. The same understanding is expressed in chapter 48 of the *Tao Te Ching*: *"Less and less do you need to force things"*.

We have all experienced those "magical" moments where everything seems to flow effortlessly, where we are participants but not directors. It could be in the playing of music, that perfect golf swing, the accomplishment of a task, a conversation, a meditative moment, a song sung, a dance danced, wood carved, communion with another. It is in the "knack" of doing something, where the something does itself, as it were.

That is the Meeting Place where, nothing forced, the energy has a life of its own, and will always align itself with the truth, with the highest purpose of who we are and what we are about.

The Meeting Place is the fundamental way we can experience the *Tao*. From that place many kinds of development are possible. The ancient Taoists, especially those focussed on spiritual alchemy, were able to experience dimensions of reality that are hard for us to imagine in our modern world. But it all started with the Meeting Place. Laozi spoke explicitly about the Meeting Place, Zhuangzi told stories about it. For the most part, amongst later Taoist adepts and thinkers, it was implicit in their work, it was assumed. We have lost awareness of this Way even though we practice it all the time.

What is so appealing about Nature, about plant life, is that we are witnessing the embodied integration of consciousness, itself the result of going to the Meeting Place. The plant's purpose is so embodied, it becomes difficult for us to imagine it has purpose. This would be a serious mistake on our part, diminishing our capacity to interact with nature. There is a cognitive process in all of nature. Remember Bertolt Brecht's dictum: *"When something seems 'the most obvious thing in the world', it means that any attempt to understand the world has been given up"*. (Bertolt Brecht, 71) The plant meets with carbon dioxide and light. As a result it grows. When we engage with life in the Meeting Place, we grow. We become more of who we are. Well-being is the result of our capacity to join consciousness with existence. We can only do this through the Meeting Place.

We can sense with a dog, for example, whether it is available for contact or not. We describe that awareness as instinct, an animal force within us that animals bring out in us. We are actually negotiating with the dog as to where the Meeting Place is, if at all. Our instincts are helpful in accessing the Meeting Place. Animals and babies invite us into the Meeting Place. The baby has no agenda, it is absolutely in the Meeting Place, and we find that invitation irresistible. In the company of a baby we can be ourselves. A baby's gaze crosses the separation we have imposed on our lives and opens the Meeting Place in our whole being. When the Dalai Lama visits, people are moved by something beyond his words. He may talk about compassion, kindness, peace or Tibet, but he is essentially without agenda, present in the Meeting Place and inviting us to join him there.

The same invitation is offered by Rumi (1207-1273 C.E.)
"Out beyond ideas of wrongdoing and right-doing,
there is a field. I'll meet you there.
When the soul lies down in that grass,
the world is too full to talk about.
Ideas, language, even the phrase: "each other"
doesn't make any sense."
(The Essential Rumi, 36)

THE MEETING PLACE OF THE BREATH

Because the breath is always present, so obvious, it is easy to remain unaware of it. We usually become aware of it when we cannot do it. What is necessary is to take the breath into a conscious process. What is happening when we breathe? Physiologically we take in oxygen, energetically we take in Qi. But what really happens to the Qi? Why, in fact, do we breathe at all?

There are two realities that explain the true significance of breathing: the Meeting Place, and Heaven and Earth. From the perspective of the ancient Chinese we are the continual manifestation or materialization of the amorous interplay of Heaven and Earth. Heaven is everything that is **infinite** about us - the sense of meaning, the imagination, our creativity, our spirituality, even our names. Our names do not change whether we are five or ninety-five, they indicate us, who are infinite. Earth is everything that is **finite** about us. It is whatever we need to do to live and function on our planet - eating, sleeping, working, our bodies. Life is the continual meeting of Heaven and Earth. Heaven cannot fulfill itself without being earthed; Earth cannot gain meaning without being infused by Heaven. Heaven and Earth are lovers constantly playing at parting and meeting.

How does the Meeting Place engage with Heaven and Earth through the breath? When we inhale, Earth is rising to meet Heaven. At the very end of the inhalation, Earth meets Heaven, Earth embraces Heaven. When we exhale, Heaven is descending to meet Earth. At the very end of the exhalation, Heaven meets Earth, Heaven embraces Earth. These two embraces, these two meetings are the most significant aspects of breathing. The Meeting Place is the place without form, therefore without limit, therefore with maximum potential. The Meeting Places of the breath are two of the most powerful connections of Heaven and Earth within us. The reason why we breathe is to embody the transformational potential of these two Meeting Places of Heaven and Earth.

What is necessary is to take the breath into a conscious process. As this conscious process, this training, continues, it starts to become a natural process again, but highly potentiated. It is a key example of consciousness joining with existence. It is a powerful way of developing 'embodied wisdom'. When practising the breath in this way, pause at the end of the inhalation and at the end of the exhalation, to allow an emphasis for these two embraces of Heaven and Earth.

When we breathe, we take in the pure essence of Heaven, inspiration, and, through the embracing power of Earth, we generate life. We can only breathe purity. With anything else we cough and splutter. In the inner, purity produces clarity and integrity; impurity produces a degradation of the human spirit. Without breath we die and yet, how often do we express our thanks to Heaven and Earth for their creation of life?

HEAVEN AND EARTH BREATHING EXERCISE

Standing position, knees slightly bent, feet shoulder-width apart, toes pointing slightly inwards, hands relaxed by your side, arms slightly apart as if a tennis ball in your armpits, tongue on the upper palate behind your teeth, breathing through your nose.

Imagine you are gathering all the cosmic qi of the universe. You gather Earth qi, that is, all that is finite about your life. What is finite is your body and everything you do to maintain your body on this plane of existence. You gather Heaven, that is, all that is infinite about you. What is infinite is everything that creates meaning in your life: love, creativity, imagination, spirituality, beauty, wonder, laughter, even your name.

Inhale and raise your arms up from the sides of your body, palms facing upward, to arc over the top of your head, palms facing down. The first half of the movement you are raising Earth qi, the second half of the movement you are raising Heaven qi. You have now gathered Earth and Heavenly qi.

Pause a moment with no breath.

Exhaling, lower your arms in front of your body as far as your belly, palms facing down. With the exhalation imagine you are breathing down the front of you into your belly all the Heaven and Earth qi you have gathered. The duration of the arm movement downwards follows the duration of your down-breath.

The front of you is your visible self, your consciousness, what you present to the world. The belly is called the Dantian and gathers qi and food to create, sustain and transform life.

Repeat two more times.

The second time, with the arms descending in front of your body, imagine you are bringing all the cosmic energy down the back of you all the way to the end of the spine. The back of you is all your invisible self, your unconsciousness, your shadow, that which is hidden from the world.

The third time, as you lower your arms down the front of your body, imagine you are bringing the cosmic energy through the core of your self, the integration of the front and the back of you, the visible and the invisible.

Then bring your feet together. Take a deep breath. Relax

THE MEETING PLACE OF THE BODY

When we eat, we take in the transformative miracle of life - putting something into our bodies from outside our bodies that, then, becomes part of us: we experience the generative power of the Earth. The ancient Chinese believe we are only hard-wired for divinely-inspired transformation - the process through which we become who we truly are. With anything less, such as the prioritization of comfort, of sentimentality, of nostalgia, of fantasy, of materialism, of the spectacle of conspicuous consumption, we find ourselves out of sync with ourselves, disengaged from the deep spirituality and generative power of the Earth, and consequently suffering a dislocation at the core. It is from this dislocation that come all our disorders, including digestive disorders. The acupuncture point at the level of the navel on the Stomach meridian, Heavenly Pivot, *Tien Shu*, is the meeting place of the generative powers of Heaven and Earth. In this meeting Heaven is grounded, Earth is inspired, and the body responds to its highest impulse: the inner and the outer, the body and the spirit, united as one. Heaven and Earth, united, result in a profound sense of relationship with our planet, with the soil beneath our feet, and with our bodies. How often do we express our thanks to the Earth for the sustenance of our life? The Earth births everything about us. Food is more than fuel: it is our experience of the absolute love and generative power of the Earth within us. Well-being is the way we relate to everything, including eating. The way we relate to eating is more important than what we eat. I am not giving a thumbs-up to junk food; I am stressing the importance of relationship. Food is not a thing, it is a meeting place of Heaven and Earth.

Written between 179-156 BCE, the *Heshang Gong* commentary on the *Tao Te Ching* says:

"The Tao of prolonged life lies with the Mysterious Female. Mysterious is heaven, within human beings it is the nose. Female is earth, within human beings it is the mouth."
(The Way of Laozi, as qtd in Kohn, 27)

We like to think of ourselves as independent adults but, without the air provided by Heaven and the food provided by Earth, we would not live very long. My teacher, J. R. Worsley, felt that a lot of disease comes from trying to be adults, or the idea that we are 'grown-up', instead of recognizing ourselves as children. By going to the Meeting Place with our planetary and heavenly parents we will naturally be thankful and respectful to life all around and within us. Eating and breathing are then in accord with Tao.

MEETING THE BODY QIGONG

Connecting with the body is connecting with the Earth within me.
The Earth element has sometimes been depicted in the centre of a circle of the other elements - Fire, Metal, Water and Fire.

It is that which grounds me.
It gives me my sense of belonging.
It connects with my digestive system through the food I ingest.

Sitting or standing,
Place your hands on your body above the navel.
With your in-breath gather nourishing qi from the Heavens.
With your down-breath, send the nourishing qi into your stomach.
With your next in-breath gather cleansing qi.
With your down breath, release a quiet singing sound - HOOOOO -
expelling stagnant qi from your digestive system into the Earth.
The Earth will recycle and transform the stagnant qi.
Repeat three times.
Do it now, right here, sitting, reading this book.

THE MEETING PLACE AND ACUPUNCTURE

"For every needling, the method is, above all,
not to miss the rooting in the Spirits"
(Neiching, chapt. 8)

There is not a place marked in the body that says 'Spirit
Here!' and yet the *Neijing* insists that we use the acupuncture
needle to connect with the *Shen*. How do I, a classically trained
acupuncturist, do that? It is through the Meeting Place. First,
there is meeting the *Shen* within me, then meeting the *Shen*
within the patient, then meeting the *Shen* within the needle,
then meeting the *Shen* in the needling itself. Everything is
aligned, the intention/attention is set, the needling can become

that spinning pivot between Heaven and Earth. There is nothing in the needle itself. It becomes an animating force through the meeting of consciousness with existence.

The process of inserting the needle into a person's body is actually the process of feeling the connection with *Wu*. In this moment *Shen* and *Wu* become synonymous. The Chinese word for the acupuncture point is *Xue*, meaning an empty, cave-like space, that is, a meaningful potential. Each *Xue* has a specific significance in the treatment process. For the classical acupuncturist the whole event of an appointment is a *Xue*, the necessity and opportunity to engage with *Wu*. The needling is only one moment in that engagement.

THE MEETING PLACE AND EFFORT

"The Tao never does anything,
but through it, everything gets done"
(Tao Te Ching. chapt. 37)

When everything flows, there is no sensation of effort. This is the experience of the Meeting Place par excellence. When we go beyond or do not reach the Meeting Place, we have gone into our minds, and then we experience effort. Moshe Feldenkrais described the sensation of effort as *"the subjective feeling of wasted movement"*, (as qtd in Cohen, 99). The difference between true movement and effort is the same difference between **suffering** (which we can handle) and the **burden** of suffering (which we cannot handle, hence illness). Effort experienced as effortful means we have gone beyond ourselves.

High levels of exertion/effort seem to be demanded of physical training regimes in the west; in contrast, eastern practices such as taiji, qigong and neigong ask practitioners to "back off" from maximum effort. It is interesting to note that the strongest position in Taiji play is the 45 degree angle of the back leg in relation to the forward position of the front leg. The back leg angled less or more than the 45 degree angle will unbalance and destabilize the body. 45 is one-eighth of the full circle of 360 degrees. So one-eighth of our energetic application will be appropriate in whatever circumstance. This will obviously vary depending on actual circumstances but as a principle it is worth observing. In our modern culture we still translate quantity as value. Giving 100% is considered the highest value. It derives from our Calvinist background. Going to the Meeting Place is a qualitative action and cannot be measured, but one-eighth sums it up nicely.

Going to the Meeting Place derives its force from within, as opposed to reacting or responding to external stimuli. As such it can draw on a limitless supply of energy since it is connected to that which has no limit. My teacher, J. R. Worsley, told me that he was as *"fresh as a daisy"* at the end of a working day, just as he was at the beginning. For me he was the real embodiment of being in the Meeting Place. In our modern world we place impossible demands on ourselves to make each day work for us, when we abandon the notion of doing, and work with meeting, life becomes effortless. What a relief when we don't have to carry the universe on our shoulders!

Through my clinic and my workshops, through my life, I hold the Meeting Place as the way to access all that is needed. It is the gateway to engage with the profound wisdom of the ancient Chinese in a way that works for us in the modern world. It is the way to engage with the wisdom and truth of ourselves. Well-being cannot be experienced without it. Going to the Meeting Place is both an inner training and a natural feature of our lives. It is accessible to us because we are alive. It does not require special knowledge or years of training, though it can lead us to specific directions for deepened exploration. We can experience it in the most mundane aspects of our lives.

And the mundane is a great way to explore it. Next time you go to the store to buy an apple, pick up the apple and feel if you can 'meet' the apple rather than just hold it. 'Meeting the apple' will let you know whether that particular apple is for you or not, even though the apple resembles all the other apples before you. We can feel the resonance between ourselves and an apple as surely as we feel it between ourselves and those we love. The mundane offers us limitless training in exploring the Meeting Place. Doesn't it feel wonderful that through holding an apple in our hand, we can experience *Tao, Wu, Shen, Yuanshen*, Heaven and Earth and *Wuwei* all at once?

A SIMPLE EXPLORATION OF THE MEETING PLACE

The next time you shake hands or hug somebody, just give the handshake or the hug the person is giving you. If their handshake is soft, let your handshake be soft. If their hug is tentative, make yours tentative.

When you do this, you are saying you have no agenda other than to meet. You will be in the Meeting Place with them. Notice what it feels like in your own body.

The larger organism of the person you are touching, will understand, will feel safe and will open appropriately, even when their ego mind has no awareness of what you are doing. The consciousness behind your consciousness and the consciousness behind their consciousness will be saying "Hello!" in the truest way possible.

Since shaking hands and hugging are normal aspects of our cultural exchanges, they are an excellent means to explore the feeling of the Meeting Place within your body.

Chapter Twelve
The Meeting Place of Inner and Outer

Living at the Meeting Place can be described as the dynamic interface of the inner and the outer - a creative tension that creates a space for something new and beneficial to occur, that is, the materialization of the *Wu*, the unknowable yet necessary mystery at the core of life and the meaning of life. In our modern culture we tend to focus on the outer, often unaware of the existence of an inner component. Without both there is no life since it is the inner that imbues the outer with life. Without the inner, the outer is dead. Without the outer, the inner cannot generate life (the transformation of energy into form).

Form is a structure that embodies the past, and we naturally create form as a way of including the past in the present. As long as form is generative and contains the potential to generate new forms, it is alive. When form fails to be generative, it fossilizes and, potentially, dies. Learning, or cognition, is life. To the extent that it is not generative, it fossilizes and potentially destroys life. The problem with our modern culture is that we have too much structure that is not generative. We have relatively inflexible work hierarchies that perpetuate themselves at the expense of the people involved in the work or even the mission of the work; we have learning environments that perpetuate themselves at the expense of the students and of the learning process; we have language structures that do not reflect the experience of the people using that language. Another example of non-generative forms and structures is mainstream Western medicine which focusses so much on the body as a series of unrelated, discreet entities, that we have a world of specializations, such as cardiac, neurological, psychiatric, with no overall context or perceptions of relationship among them all. The overall context and the understanding of relationship in the body will naturally develop generative language, generative thought and generative practice appropriate to this context and this relationship. The examination of human life through the generative theme of the Taoist Five Elements, for example, gives context to form and creates diagnostic and treatment processes that acknowledge the integrity and dynamic nature of life. It is the reason why classical acupuncture has been described as "life meeting life".

There is value in the acknowledgment and examination of structure. That is not a problem or an issue. The issue is that structures that are non-generative, that is, structures that do not reflect reality or, as the ancients say, true principles, and therefore do not create a response of vitality within us. Non-generative structures do not nourish our spirit, our *Shen*. Generative structures will always create something new, some new unfolding of the movement of life within us. Because our everyday lives are filled with many non-generative activities and attitudes that do not nourish our *Shen*, we have set aside times and places - the weekend, the holiday, the retreat - for recreation and generation of an inner life. We have even set up specific arenas for different parts of ourselves. In the field of healing we have sent our bodies to doctors, our minds to psychiatrists and our spirits to guides, gurus and religions.

The displacement of millions of people on our planet at this time is matched by a displacement at the heart of our modern culture and our modern psyches. The long-term subordination of content (the human spirit) to form (social controls) has resulted in severe non-generative structures (imperialism, war, environmental degradation, patriarchy). As a result, we are facing a crisis of planetary life beyond anything we have experienced before, as I said in the opening chapter. The consequence is that, increasingly, nobody belongs anywhere anymore... but we all want to. We all want that balance of inner and outer because their relationship is life generating itself.

Belonging is as much a part of us as breathing. If we cannot belong in our authentic life, we will find somewhere else to belong, because we cannot live without belonging. The separation of the inner from the outer produces an existential loneliness - we are, therefore we are lonely. We can be easily tempted by homes of temporary distraction or inauthentic belonging - dominant cultural practices, groups, consumer experiences, gurus, authorities, beliefs, amusements, addictions. Inauthentic belonging is based on the submission of the unique inner part of ourselves to something outside us, for example, external state authority, or to pre-existing external structures, for example, family expectations. Unfortunately, inauthentic belonging provides no generative meeting place between the inner and the outer, or the individual and the community.

Belonging is a significant experience of living in the Meeting Place. When we are in the Meeting Place, we feel connected and appropriate. In the Meeting Place - the place of no agenda, of no predefined form, and, therefore, of maximum potential - we connect with who we really our, that is, what the ancients call our original nature, *Yuanshen*. *Yuanshen* is the truth of ourselves - the place of belonging at the deepest level of meaning - and is the experience of *Tao*. When we engage in the practice of going to the Meeting Place, we meet with a felt experience in our bodies. As a result of meeting with the felt experience of our bodies, and patiently focussing on the creative tension held in that meeting, we allow space for the mystery, the *Wu*, at the core of us, to sort things out in accordance with our original nature. This process of allowing the *Wu* the space it needs in our bodies, results in a harmony of inner and outer. It is the dynamic harmony of inner and outer that produces a sense of belonging - of being fundamentally in the process of relationship with ourselves and everything that is.

Failed attempts at healing the rift between our inner and outer lives in our culture, have resulted in pathologies such as obesity, depression, or self-medication. Obesity in North America has reached epidemic proportions. One in three is obese. It has been suggested that half the adult population of the United States is using anti-depressants. Overeating and overmedication help anaesthetize the terror and anxiety at the root of our displaced selves, the result of not being in our authentic balance of inner and outer. Overeating is based on a retreat into the infantile, where being filled up like a baby at the breast of the mother means everything is OK and we can avoid the terror of aloneness and existential disconnect. Similarly, the light and love focus of New Agism, where there is no shadow, no underbelly, no edge, where bliss is the retreat into the womb, is a compensation for and a manifestation of the terror and anxiety at the root of the homeless soul.

We experience belonging when inner and outer are in relationship, that is, in the Meeting Place. Going to the Meeting Place of the inner and the outer allows us to break through what the Taoists called "acquired conditioning" and connect with our authentic self. Acquired conditioning is the biographical triumph of survival over our selves and at the same time the challenge to manifest our authentic nature. Acquired conditioning is what is "in" us but not "of" us. We experience it in our body when we feel claustrophobic, stuck, depressed, clumsy, forgetful, tense, breathless, fearful, overheated, lacking in confidence and anxious. We feel narrower, heavier, darker, less. It is the experience of not being in the Meeting Place, but in a state ruled by pre-defined agendas that eat away at our sense of identity.

The inner wisdom and practice of the ancient Chinese, expressed in the experience of the Meeting Place, can lead us back to a sense of self as relationship. When we are in relationship with ourselves, we are no longer lonely, no longer absent from our own lives. When we "belong" at the core of ourselves, not only can we belong anywhere, but also we will naturally generate structures of belonging, for example, in the design of homes and towns, in the codifying of laws, in the components of health care.

"Let the Tao be present in your life
and you will become genuine.
Let it be present in your family

and your family will flourish.
Let it be present in your country
and your country will be an example.
Let it be present in the universe
and the universe will sing.
How do I know this is true?
By looking inside myself."

(Tao Te Ching, chapt. 54, trans. Mitchell)

EMBODIED WISDOM - THE INCARNATION OF INNER AND OUTER THROUGH THE MEETING PLACE

Another way of describing the Meeting Place, in its interface of inner and outer, is the interface of yin and yang. In the outer, yang represents our capacity to generate consciousness. In the inner, yin represents our capacity to integrate that consciousness within our bodies, the dynamics of which process generate new and richer capacity for consciousness. The ancients say we need true practices that help anchor our knowing in our cellular structure, thereby creating the endless transformations that direct us towards our destinies, to who we really are. Qigong, taiji, classical acupuncture and other practices are all Meeting Places where knowing and cellular structure interpenetrate and expand one another. Through the Meeting Place we can potentiate the relationship of knowing and cellular structure, and support the generation of embodied consciousness or embodied wisdom. For the ancient Chinese, Knowing-How, or *Zhi*, is the manifestation of embodied consciousness.

"When something takes charge of being alive,
we speak of the Heart.
When the Heart applies itself,
we speak of Intent.
When Intent becomes permanent,
we speak of Will.
When the persevering Will changes,
we speak of Thought.
When Thought extends itself powerfully and far,
we speak of Reflection.
When Reflection can have all beings at its disposal,
we speak of Knowing-How."
(Neijing Lingshu, chapt. 8)

 Zhi, "Knowing-How" encompasses elements that are two sides of the same coin - longevity and freedom. Longevity comprises two aspects - the nourishment of our finite physical life on earth, and living according to eternal principles, that is according to what is infinite about us. Freedom is the result of mastering the mind and closely relating the mind to natural rather than conditioned responses, thereby opening us up to an authentic life. The twin focus on longevity and freedom produces Knowing-How. Knowing-How is the state of mastery and the state of embodied wisdom. Embodied wisdom is the goal of all ancient methods and trainings.

The ancient Chinese were not interested in forms of physical calisthenics. They were much more interested in physical activities that could produce an embodied wisdom, a wisdom expressing itself in the cells of the body itself; a wisdom that reflected cosmic reality. Whatever is "out there" is also "in here" and whatever is "in here" is "out there". It is all one. This oneness the Chinese called *Tian*, Heaven.

Embodied wisdom means that thought, feeling and action, including the poise and movement of the body and the rhythm and expression of the breath, flow from a knowing residing within the body and result in a capacity to be truly present in every situation we face, including death and dying. This capacity is what the Chinese meant by our term "Health".

Health practices such as qigong and taiji can certainly strengthen the physical body, but their primary purpose is to potentiate an already existing capacity in human beings - the capacity to transform energy into embodied wisdom. This natural capacity, when consciously supported, is known as spiritual alchemy. Zhang Sanfeng hints at this when he says:

"Clearly discriminate the Substantial and Insubstantial.
There is an aspect of Substantial and Insubstantial
in every part of the body.
Considered in their entirety,
all things have this nature."
(T'ai Chi According to the I Ching, Stuart Alve Olson, Rochester, Inner Traditions, 2001)

The ancients imagined an alchemical container using the ingredients of the three treasures, *Jing, Qi* and *Shen*, to provide the mix for transformation. *Jing, Qi,* and *Shen* can be translated in this instance as Body, Breath and Intention. This alchemical container was understood to reside in the fields of potential in the body - the *Dantians*, especially the lower *Dantian* residing in the belly below the navel. The alignment of the body, the breath and the intention incorporated into all practices of qigong, neigong and taiji, create the meeting place for the invitation to the *Wu* to manifest more clearly in the individual practitioner through the *Dantian*, and potentiate the process of embodying wisdom at the cellular level.

Alchemical transformation by the *Wu* via the *Dantian* - the meeting place of the three treasures (*Jing, Qi* and *Shen*) - results in greater embodied wisdom. Embodied wisdom is the embodiment of "the force that guides" mentioned in the Introduction. It is embodied wisdom that produced the 'knowing' in the ancients which then produced forms of activities such as qigong and taiji. When we practice a particular form of qigong or taiji, we can feel the live energy within the form. It is a generative form. The ancients understood this and, at the same time, tried not to 'fossilize' the forms being generated. The Taoists knew this would cause non-generative structure. There is a Zen story which reflects this:

A Zen Master tells his student that he has accomplished all that he, the Master, can teach, and is now worthy to establish his own teaching. The Zen Master offers as a gift of parting a book which contains not only his insights about the training, but also the insights of his teacher and his teacher's teacher. The student refuses to take it. The Master insists. The student takes it and throws it in the fire. "What are you doing!", screams the Master. "What are you saying?" asks the student."

While they respected the forms that were produced, they always recognized these forms as manifestations of something else - internal alchemy. My acupuncture teacher, J. R. Worsley, recognized this truth in the practice of acupuncture when he once said, "There are no churches in acupuncture". The Meeting Place has many uses and is most useful in supporting us to find that fine balance between energy and structure in all areas of body, mind and spirit, and in all areas of life. The best form of taiji or qigong for you is the one through which you feel your energy rise, and where you feel lighter, brighter, clearer, more - in other words, where you are in the Meeting Place. The evidence of its appropriateness is always in the felt experience of your body.

In ancient China there was no such term as qigong. This word has been created to get below the radar of communist censorship in China. The umbrella term for all the practices that engage with *Wu* is *Yangsheng* - nourishing life. Doesn't that sound more appealing than 'energy work' or 'putting energy into practice', the actual meaning of qigong? *Yangsheng*, nourishing life, is what it's all about, and is the closest equivalent to our phrase, well-being.

How do we read ourselves when we are in a form of crisis? It might be a physical ailment, it might be a mental issue, it might be an issue of the spirit. Our tendency is to look at it as a negative. After all, it is usually uncomfortable, possibly painful. It could feel like an emotional roller-coaster. We could feel drained of energy, without initiative, without spark. We could find ourselves going into a state of despair, a sense of hopelessness, or at least confusion, lethargy or forgetfulness. How many patients have I seen where versions of these are manifesting? Answer - many. Why? Are we just collapsing? Is life basically impossible? The answer is no, we are not collapsing. We are going through the process of transformation and healing. Illness or crisis is often the initial, sometimes continuing, way we use to earth ourselves, to ground ourselves in reality. It involves a gentle or dramatic shake-up that dissolves whatever certainties and expectations we have imposed on our lives. These certainties and expectations are the agenda that comes from acquired conditioning. They constitute an imbalance of form over energy, of *Ke* over *Sheng* in the dynamic of the five elements. When we have crisis, we find we take nothing for granted. Nothing is obvious anymore. As a result, we are in a very creative state, open, more vulnerable, more receptive, very fluid and more available to go to the Meeting Place.

When we have a crisis, we have gone to depth and find ourselves in the oftentimes unfamiliar landscape of the inner. A crisis is the result of a disconnect between our inner and outer lives. Our bodies, faithful servants to our destinies that they are, take us to depth so that we can start to connect with who we truly are. The problem is that we view the experience as negative because it is uncomfortable, because in our past we have only experienced depth negatively as suffering, and because we make a judgement on ourselves, that somehow we are failing. We see ourselves failing because we have an agenda about how we should be, which seldom corresponds to how we actually are. The judgement on ourselves is the result of the acquired conditioning we have gone through in our lives. The judgement on ourselves is also the place where we can start to unravel the knots around our own suffering, to liberate our suffering from its burden. Behind the judgement there is a virtue. If we feel useless in ourselves, for example, it is because we are asking: What is useful? What does it mean to be useful? This is the virtue. When we stay with the self-criticism, in this instance a form of self-abuse, we stay with the acquired conditioning, and are unable to engage the Meeting Place.

The materialism of the modern world has penetrated all areas of life - from science to spirituality - and banished the inner experience and the necessity of integration to the dark shadowlands. The irrepressible force for integration within us, however, is resistant and resisting, demanding more attention. It is why you are reading these words. We want an integrated life where all parts of us are unified according to our natures. We need to re-define what our suffering is all about. The ancient Taoists, those wise men and women whose focus transcended historical time, can be great resources for us as we navigate our way through our lives towards a new dynamic of well-being. The essence, the core, of this navigation is through the Meeting Place. The Meeting Place is both a place and a pro-

cess. We are on a pilgrimage called our life and as our wonderful friend, Rumi, says, *"This is not a caravan of despair"*. (*Rumi,
The Illuminated Rumi,* 3). The Meeting Place offers us the
access to this caravan and, at the same time, begins the process
of healing and transformation that we all ache for, deep within
ourselves.

EPILOGUE

This book started as a response to a question by a participant in one of my Tao of Wellbeing seminars in England. The question was - where is the book? I realized that what I was exploring in my groups, although hinted at, referred to, acknowledged, had never been, to my knowledge, a focus of a book. So this book is an attempt to start filling a gap. The perspective and methodology of the Meeting Place not only provide a unifying theme underlying all ancient Taoist practice, but also provide a way for us in the twenty-first century to connect with the ancient wisdom in ways that are accessible, practical and immediate. Even more importantly, the Meeting Place provides a way to embody the ancient wisdom at the cellular level. Embodying wisdom is the practice of well being and the Meeting Place is the process of that practice.

The truth is that we all practise and have practised the Meeting Place all our lives. However, the practice has either been unconscious, or identified under the umbrella of instinct and intuition. It has not been identified as a practical method of engagement with reality. Until now it has not been named for what it is - the Meeting Place. The Meeting Place provides a unifying golden thread through every aspect of our lives. At the same time it helps make sense of Taoist thought. And it helps shift the conversation about well-being away from outcomes to process, to Zhuangzi's 'force that guides'. The Meeting Place is a generative process, able to engage us in every aspect of our lives in a way which enlivens us and helps us stay true to reality, to true principles.

There are already established practices from inner traditions which provide mechanisms of engagement with reality, such as meditation, prayer, fasting, silent retreat, teachings, music, chants and sound, charity, pilgrimage. The Meeting Place is the most potent way to engage with all these practices. It is the practice within the practice, the consciousness within the consciousness. By meeting these practices, as opposed to 'doing' them, we release a dynamic that is at the heart of all the teachings of the inner traditions. As St. Francis of Assisi said, *"What you are looking for, is what is looking"*.

This book is not complete and could never be. The implications of the Meeting Place are vast. The generative process that it powers gives direct felt experience of ideas such as 'tao', 'field of potential', 'reality', 'health', 'well-being' and anything we have yet to understand or acknowledge. It is a finger pointing in a certain direction. That direction emphasizes the role of experience inside the body as a way of knowing something. That thought is not new, but the self-training process of the Meeting Place within the body is new. That direction provides a dynamic through which new insight can come and also a dynamic that allows the human body to sort itself out in ways that are appropriate, authentic and life-strengthening. In addition, the Meeting Place is a way to strengthen the centrality of the mystery in the midst of the 'known' world, the no-thing within the some-thing.

"what is above form is called Tao"
(I Ching, 323)

— 134 —

"It is the great virtue of Heaven and Earth to bestow life.
It is the great treasure of the holy sage to stand in the right place."
(I Ching, 328)

The Meeting Place engages Wu.
Engaged with Wu, we experience Tao.
Experiencing Tao, we are Well-Being.

The Meeting Place does not exist until you go there.
It has no form.
Without form it has no limit.
Without limit it has maximum potential.
The Meeting Place is everywhere.

GLOSSARY OF CHINESE WORDS

Chung-kuo the Middle Kingdom

dantian 'cinnabar field'.

There are three dantian - upper, middle, lower. Generally used term to indicate the lower cinnabar field below the navel. Cinnabar, a result of mixing sulphuric and mercurial components, comes from the work of the early alchemists and here indicates the place of transformation where air and food are transformed into life within us, but also the inner process of change where life becomes destiny.

Hua the flowery, splendid people of ancient China

*Huangd*i the Yellow Emperor, legendary author of the Neiching, supposed creator of medicine

huo the fire element of the five elements

hun the non-corporeal soul; the visionary imagination within us that embraces our destiny; the way of being in community without losing our uniqueness; the inner dimension of the wood element

jin the metal element of the five elements

jing the earthly essence

k'o the control cycle of the five elements

Laozi legendary author of the *Tao Te Ching*, the ancient Taoist classic

ming destiny

mu the wood element of the five elements

Neiching the most ancient Chinese medical classic

po the corporeal soul; the capacity to recognize all

	life as precious; embodied wisdom; our capacity to be inspired; the inner dimension of the metal element
Qibo	the physician-consultant to Huangdi, the Yellow Emperor
shao yin	the heart and kidney meridians on the body
shen	the spirits or heavenly forces, agents of the wu, who reside in the heart, radiant and sparking life
shen	our capacity to stand in the now, the present moment, where our horizontal temporal reality intersects with our vertical eternal reality; where we find our capacity for love; the inner dimension of the fire element
shenzi	the acquired personality
sheng	the life cycle, or creative cycle of the five elements
shui	the water element of the five elements
tao	a way of being in accord with reality or 'true principles"
tien shu	Heavenly Pivot, acupuncture point on the Stomach meridian
tu	the Earth element of the five elements
xin	the heart-mind
Xi Wang Mu	Queen Mother of the West, Earth Goddess, "the darkest cavern of the psyche" (Dechar, *Five Spirits*)
wu	the unknowable, unnameable mystery at the centre of life; the number five; the pre-Taoist ancient shamans of neolithic China
wuxing	the five elements
wushen	the inner dimension of the five elements
wuwei	knowing without knowing
yi	intention; to establish 'meaning in the world with words that come from the heart' (Jarrett, Nourishing Destiny); the process of embodying wisdom; it makes the possibility of

	change available; the inner dimension of the earth element
yin yang	the dynamic equilibrium of complementary opposites
yuanshen	original true nature or spirit of a person
zhenqi	authentic self or energy
zhi	knowing-how; wisdom - the capacity to find something enduring amidst the transience of life; the capacity to surrender to the deepest truths of our original nature; the inner dimension of the water element
Zhuangzi	Fourth Century B.C.E. The most famous Taoist after Laozi

BIBLIOGRAPHY

Brecht, Bertolt. *Brecht on Brecht*. Trans. John Willett. New York: Hill and Wang, 1964. Print

Capra, Fritjof and Luisi, Pier Luigi. *A Systems View of Life*. Cambridge: Cambridge University Press, 2014. Print.

Chang Po-tuan. *The Inner Teachings of Taoism*. Trans.Thomas Cleary. Boston: Shambhala Publications, 1986. Print.

Chang Po-tuan. *Understanding Reality*. Trans. Thomas Cleary. Honolulu: University of Hawaii Press, 1987. Print.

Cohen, Kenneth S. *The Way of Qigong*. New York: Ballentine Books, 1997. Print

Dechar, Lorie Eve. *Five Spirits*. New York: Lantern Books, 2006. Print.

Jarrett, Lonny S. *Nourishing Destiny*. Stockbridge: Spirit Path Press,, 2004. Print.

Johnson, Professor Jerry Alan. *Chinese Medical Qigong Therapy, Vol.1*. Pacific Grove: The International Institute of Medical Qigong, 2005. Print.

Jung, C.G. *Memories, Dreams and Reflections*. London: Fontana Paperbacks, 1989. Print.

Katie, Byron. *A Thousand Names for Joy.* New York: Three Rivers Press, 2007. Print.

Kohn, Livia. *Early Chinese Mysticism.* Princeton: Princeton University Press, 1992. Print

Larre, Claude and Rochat de la Vallee, Elisabeth, Schatz, Jean. *Survey of Traditional Chinese Medicine.* Columbia: Traditional Acupuncture Foundation and L'Institut Ricci, 1986. Print.

Larre, Claude and Rochat de la Vallee, Elisabeth. *The Heart.* Cambridge: Monkey Press, 1991. Print.

Larre, Claude and Rochat de la Vallee, Elisabeth. *Rooted in Spirit.* New York: Station Hill Press, 1992. Print.

Larre, Claude and Rochat de la Vallee, Elisabeth. *The Seven Emotions.* Cambridge: Monkey Press, 1996. Print.

Marx, Karl. *The 18th Brumaire of Louis Bonaparte.* New York: Wildside Press LLC, 2008. Print

Mitchell, Stephen. *The Essence of Wisdom.* New York: Broadway Books, 1998. Print.

Olson, Stuart Alve. *T'ai Chi According to the I Ching.* Rochester: Inner Traditions, 2001. Print.

Rumi. *The Essential Rumi.* Trans. Coleman Barks. New York: HarperCollins, 1996. Print.

Rumi. *The Illuminated Rumi.* Trans. Coleman Barks. New York: Broadway Books, 1997. Print

Tao Te Ching. Trans. Stephen Mitchell. New York: HarperPerennial, 1991. Print.

Tao Te Ching Lao-Tzu. Trans. Stephen Addiss and Stanley Lombardo. Boston: Hackett Publishing,1993. Print.

Taoist Meditation. Trans. Thomas Cleary. Boston: Shambhala Publications, 2000. Print.

The I Ching or Book of Changes. Trans. Richard Wilhelm. Princeton: Princeton University Press, 1967. Print.

The Second Book of the Tao. Trans. Stephen Mitchell. New York: Penguin Books, 2009. Print.

The Taoist I Ching. Trans. Thomas Cleary. Boston: Shambhala Publications, 1986. Print.

The Way of Laozi. Trans. Wing-tsit Chan. Princeton: Prentice Hall, 1963. Print.

The Yellow Emperor's Classic of Internal Medicine. Trans. Ilza Veith. University of California Press, December, 2002. Print.

Thomas, Dylan. *Dylan Thomas, Selected Poems 1934 - 1952.* New York: New Directions, 1952. Print.

Worsley, J.R. *Classical Five-Element Acupuncture Volume III.* Worsley, J.R. and J.B. Publications. 1988. Print.